Tammy,

I wish you a "profitable" life
filled with love and laughter.

Leslie

Dating Our Money

A Women's Guide To Confidence With Money and Men

Leslie Greenman

authorHOUSE®

AuthorHouse™
1663 Liberty Drive
Bloomington, IN 47403
www.authorhouse.com
Phone: 1-800-839-8640

Published by AuthorHouse   01/12/2012

ISBN: 978-1-4634-1740-6 (sc)
ISBN: 978-1-4634-1742-0 (hc)
ISBN: 978-1-4634-1741-3 (e)

Library of Congress Control Number: 2011909167

To My Two Cool Kids

Ben and Luke

Thank you for teaching me the true meaning

of unconditional love and being fearless!

Your smiles and hugs can wipe away any sadness.

I am glad you are my number one fans and

I hope you know I always want to cheer

you on and push you to be your best.

Plus

A Heartfelt Gratitude

To

My Mother and Sister

Who have stood by my side

And

Kept encouraging me even in my lowest moments.

Thank you!

Table of Contents

Introduction

"What can you accomplish this year if you
*take **fear** out of your vocabulary?"*

- Janice Pellar,

Emco Technologies

Dating Our Money. Rarely do we see the words dating and money put together. Yet, each of these two words has created countless heartaches, headaches, and hopefully, happiness for women. When writing this book, I wanted to show you don't have to be an expert with money to dip your feet in—just like no one is truly an expert at dating. We get better and better at dating over time, but it definitely comes with many rough moments.

Budgeting and managing money is the same. We all have made money mistakes and done stupid things that can often get us in trouble but NO course is irreversible. With the right knowledge and attitude, both money and men can be an enjoyable and wonderful part of our lives. It is important to learn how to keep both of them in balance. Anything in life is harmful if it gets out of balance. This is definitely true of money and men!

Men love to share their scary experiences with dating certain women in the past. Almost every story a guy will share about a crazy ex has to do with someone not letting go and thinking that with an extreme display of affection they can change the other person. Does this ever work? NO! Neither does going out on a wild shopping spree to solve our depression. Yes, it may bring momentary joy, even when our credit cards are almost maxed out; but it never solves the true problem. Honestly, eating a pint of ice cream would probably be a better answer because one can work that off at the gym much quicker than one can get oneself out of credit card debt.

Together, we are going to look at destructive patterns of behavior that need to be eliminated in order to make room for our true, beautiful, powerful selves to emerge.

Countless men have told me they quit dating a woman because of her wild spending habits, total disregard for saving money, and her lack of ability to live within a budget. Most men don't want to be anyone's ATM. Women, impulsive buying may not only be ruining our wallets, it may also be harming our love life.

It is hard enough to find a good man, so let's NOT make money the obstacle to true happiness. Simple changes in our spending and saving habits can create a whole new future for us. Now, I need your help!

This book is a journey-a journey that I want us to take together. I have always imagined this book to be like "Sex in the City" meets financial planning. Together, I want us to learn and laugh. This book demands your involvement. It requires each of us to be honest with ourselves. We need to search our past and present to perceive what we have done well with money and men. This gives us a launching pad so we know how to develop plans for the future. What do we need to change? Where are we displaying destructive patterns of behavior such as spending more than we make? These bad habits need to stop *NOW*, and we can do it together!

Together, we are going to create a roadmap for our futures. If we know exactly what our goals are, then it will be clear what relationships fit with our purpose in life. We will know very quickly after meeting a man if he wants to be our cheerleader and push us forward or if he is going to drag us down in his financial and emotional debt. We will discuss the danger of emotional baggage, because that is a very real concept, especially after painful divorces!

On my desk is a bumper sticker from W.I.F.E. (Women in Financial Education) that states "A Man is Not a Financial Plan." I love this idea because we often believe that a man will bring us happiness, stability and financial freedom. Please take off your rose colored glasses. Often a man comes with more financial baggage then we ever had or expected. The problem lies within us. We are in so much fear of starting over that we stay in a relationship when in our heart we know it is wrong. Don't worry. All of us have been there, and this book is full of stories to comfort each of us. You are not alone! To have true happiness, you must have financial *AND* emotional peace.

My friend is registered on the website wealthymen.com. My girlfriends and I have had a few good laughs looking over her recent matches and seeing that honestly this is not the place to meet your true prince charming. Wake up. There is no prince charming. No man is out there to save you. You need to save yourself. A man can help provide emotional and physical support, but you have to bring yourself as an equal to the relationship. If you don't bring emotional and financial security to the table, you will be in a position where a man may try to dominate you. I would never want that for any woman. This book teaches women how to take back control so they can be financial and emotional equals whether with partners or alone.

Money is the number one reason for divorce in America.

You cannot ignore a man's spending habits. Are they in line with yours? What do you see as potential conflicts down the road? Do you agree on how to manage money and save for the future? Don't ignore the red flags if you are not on the same page. This is *SO* important. I definitely have broken up with or never started dating certain men because I have seen signs of poor money management in their past.

Let's learn to trust our gut with money and men. STOP. Don't get into another relationship until you have an honest look at how you manage money in and out of relationships. See what characteristics to look for in men that show they can handle their money responsibly. My friends laugh at me because I will usually know by the second date almost everything about how my date views money—even their credit score—without asking one direct question. In this book, I will teach you methods to protect yourself from someone who will ruin your life— emotionally and financially.

Being alone is better than being in a bad relationship, but I also know how much courage and confidence it takes to stand alone. It is not easy! As a financial planner, I help a lot of women with money. Over and over, I hear a story about husbands who have walked out and left women penniless and powerless. These men are smart and have hidden money in overseas bank accounts, or in cash, where the courts cannot find it. This has left women broke emotionally and financially. They feel helpless. Their world has been turned upside down overnight, and it takes a long time to pick up the pieces and start again. They usually need to adapt to a totally new lifestyle and often sell their home. Let's stop this cycle! Women need to educate themselves and become as financially savvy as men. Let's be real for a moment—men are no smarter with money than women. They are just good at putting on that façade.

Why do I care so much about this topic? My life changed overnight when my husband unexpectedly passed on at 35. Suddenly, I became a single parent of two ACTIVE boys, both under four years old at the time. Within a few months, I had to sell my special events and catering businesses, which I had owned for over ten years, because it required me to work frequent nights and weekends. If I had stayed in my business, most of the profits would have been eaten up with babysitting and daycare expenses. I also decided to sell my house and move to another state where I had family nearby.

It was tough leaving behind a wonderful home my husband and I had built less than two years before as well as leaving long-time friends. I left behind my support system—meaning my friends and co-workers who had helped me through the toughest times I had faced. My father had died completely unexpectedly in the night when I was a sophomore in high school. From that point on, my mom lectured me to be very independent and never completely rely on a man for support, because you never know what will happen. Still my husband's death caught me by surprise. You always think it will never happen to you. I am living proof that it can! That doesn't mean it has to destroy you.

You have a choice. I made the choice to live for my children and never spend time dwelling on the "what if" questions that can consume you. I had to live in the NOW for my kids and be grateful that I still had two happy, healthy children. I had to become a role model for my kids showing that you can move forward through tough times and grow stronger.

My big regret is that my husband and I never discussed money. He hated talking about budgets, and I didn't want to ruffle the feathers in our household, so I stayed quiet. Now I know I was wrong. Our life would have been so different if I had had a "voice" in that relationship and stood my ground. He didn't believe in life insurance, so I listened to him. Now, I know how different our life would have been if we had bought a life insurance policy. He said he had a Will, but we never found it. The list goes on. I can't change the past, but I can change the future. That is why I am here. I have become smarter and wiser now. Women, it is time to wake up! Your husband or boyfriend doesn't have ALL the right answers about ways to do things. You need to educate yourself.

After my husband passed on, I started giving seminars entitled, "Where there is a <u>Will</u>, there is a Way." I was the personal story in the talk and then I had an attorney, financial planner, real estate agent and mortgage broker speak. People soon expected that I had all the answers to their money issues, so I studied endlessly and earned the licenses I needed to be a financial advisor. Now I can help women prepare for the unexpected curveballs that life throws them. Again, I want to empower women to take the time to teach themselves about how to wisely manage their money. It takes time and discipline. These are qualities you need to use in all aspects of your life, including dating. It is so easy to fall for the first guy you meet after something traumatic happens in your life. You owe it to yourself to take the time to date around and see what else is out there. Also, you need to value your time and learn quickly what is worth making the effort for and what is not. Time is a finite resource we can't get back, so discipline is essential.

The first financial article I wrote was entitled, "Don't date a guy who drives a Porsche. Like a slick financial advisor, he will speed in and out of your life." Unfortunately, this article came from real life experience! Yes, we have to learn tough lessons. Either I was going to cry and kick myself for making a stupid mistake, or I could decide to laugh, learn the lessons and move on. As a result, this book was born. It is my gift to women. It is okay to be picky and smart about your choices with money and men. The consequences can be life-altering and life-shattering if you don't take the time to learn about money and men. I have finally found my voice and learned to speak honestly and openly. Now, I want you to do the same. It will change the course of your life!

Women need to have a voice with managing money! They have valuable skills to add. The Christian Science Monitor newspaper printed an article entitled "More women in finance, more sustainable economy" which was very insightful. It discussed how more women are needed in finance. Studies show most of the recent financial scandals would have been avoided if there had been more women in upper levels of the financial industry. Women are less impulsive and results oriented so they help balance the business model. Catalyst, a non-profit organization that tracks women in business, shows that "companies with more gender-diverse boards outperform companies with non-diverse boards by 53 percent." The research goes even further to show "companies with the most gender diversity among employees bring in nearly $600 million more in sales revenue than companies that lack gender diversity." Hooray! Let's help spread the word. Women are powerful and needed even in the business world.

A "good old boys club" still exists in some financial institutions. In my first job, I was the only woman in the office. I heard more about strip clubs and sports than I need to know for the rest of my life. I am a single parent and one day my boss said to me, "If the market was crashing and your children's school called because your child was sick, I know you would go after your child. I need someone who will stay here no matter what." It was time to go, because I had never lied about being a single parent. I was grateful that a new job had already opened up that gave me the flexibility I needed and was a fun, healthy atmosphere.

Work environments can be no different than relationships. Initially, I was grateful when this first job opened up. It seemed like an answer to my prayers and my boss said that I was an answer to his need. See how quickly things can change? That is true with relationships, also. We think we have finally found "the one" and we are relieved because the search is finally over. No more dating. Hooray! (We all know dating sucks!) Yet, in a few months, a bad feeling develops in the bottom of our stomach. We try to ignore it, saying this is much better than being alone, but the nagging feeling won't go away. It is time to stop, get real, and be honest. Have the courage to believe in your self and walk away. It is okay to be picky! Please don't settle, because you will never be happy in the long run. Don't let his sweet words change your decision. The <u>only</u> person that you need to make happy is yourself. Women, it is time to realize you have a right to not settle. A healthy relationship won't develop from it!

Am I relationship expert? No, but I have learned a lot sitting across from couples creating a financial plan for their future. I can see how different people react when confronted with touchy questions like, "How would you like your assets to be distributed if your husband remarried after your death?" People squirm, and you learn a lot about how emotionally and financially mature people behave. You learn if they handle money as a couple, or if one person dominates. The whole goal of this book is to empower women to take control of their financial and emotional lives!

If you are married, now is the time to make sure you are an equal partner. What would happen if your spouse passed on or became disabled tomorrow? Would you know how to manage and pay all the household expenses? Could you maintain your current lifestyle, or would you need to sell your house or change jobs? You need to know the answer to all these questions and many more!

If you are single, you need to be honest. Do I have a budget? No, a mental budget is not the answer you need! What is keeping you from creating a budget and living within your means? How can you change this? Saving money saves lives! Later in this book, we will discuss how saving money could be a safety rope in your life. It can protect you even in the worst of situations.

Thank you for deciding to share this journey with me. Together we will change and grow together. I know I am a different person now than when I started the process of writing this book. Each step has made me stop and reevaluate my life. I hope it provokes the same response for you and encourages you to grow and learn. You can never learn too much about money and men!!!!!!

1

Let's Get Real . . . NOW!

"If you do not find peace in yourself,
you will never find it anywhere else."

                        - Paula A. Bendry

Honesty is a hard thing to find both in the dating world and the financial industry, as we read in the news headlines. In this book I promise to be perfectly honest with you and share my horrific dating stories and the stupid money mistakes I have made, in hopes of our learning many valuable lessons together. Now, I need a commitment from you to value your time. Instead of going on another stupid date that is going to go nowhere, I want you to take the time to invest in YOURSELF. Right now you need to stop and evaluate your life. What have you done well with money and men? What lessons could you learn before going into your next relationship, so you enter it feeling confident and powerful?

Good or bad . . . money is power. I may be wrong, but I don't think anyone became the friend of a powerful businessman solely because he has a winning personality. Those in power want to learn and be around others who are powerful and influential. Don't we all at times? No, I don't think your goal in life should be to become a business magnate, but I use this example to illustrate a point. We all need to recognize that money can be a valuable resource in helping us to gain equality or power when we enter relationships. Knowing how to manage your money and having financial peace will give you confidence. Women get abused in relationships and at work when they feel trapped and think there is no way out. The knowledge we gain together can protect us from this point forward. You can live confidently knowing you are any man's equal. Don't let anyone abuse you— emotionally or physically. Either one is dangerous.

What is the number one trait that men find attractive in women? Confidence! This book is going to help you attract the right kind of people into your life. I will help you see the warning signs about who you don't want in your life. Don't worry. I have made plenty of mistakes myself. Ask my friends. They have shared my tears and laughter with each new dating saga and lesson learned.

Ok, now it is time to stop and take a tough look at ourselves. (It is okay to get up and look at your beautiful self in the mirror while you ask yourself these questions.)

A PERSONAL EVALUATION

1. **Where are you at this stage in life?**

2. **Have you reached your goals?**

3. **Are you in a good place financially and emotionally?**

4. **What would you like to change from this point forth?**

Read my answers to these questions to see if they give you some guidance:

1. **Where are you at this stage in life?**

I am a single parent who has finally learned how to be comfortable being alone and confident in speaking the truth. When my husband passed on, it was very hard at first to go to functions by myself. I felt self-conscious because everyone else was married, but now I am okay with being alone. (Not that I wouldn't rather have the perfect date, but I have quickly learned that no date is better than a BAD date!)

I adore being a mother, but I also fear what will happen as my boys grow older and less dependent on me. Right now, my whole life is centered around them and their activities, while trying to juggle work.

2. **Have you reached your goals?**

Are you crazy? Of course not! Work is where I feel I fall short most recently, and it is hard for me because I want to give my all to everything I do. I know everyone has to pick different priorities at different stages of life and right now, being a mom comes first. It still eats at me because I want to be successful with my career too. My mom lectures me, "You won't get these years back. Enjoy your time with the kids. It will be gone before you know it."

3. Are you in a good place emotionally and financially?

The answer depends on the day and time of day that you ask. Are my boys body slamming each other and driving me crazy, or are they cuddling with me and saying, "You are the best mom ever."

Overall I am grateful. I have a loving family and friends who have absolutely been there for me through the good and bad. I hope everyone reading this book has a strong support system because you will need it at some point in your life. If you are in a relationship that has isolated you from all your friends and family, this is a huge red flag. Please get out now. You can't go it alone, and you will become resentful of your boyfriend or husband. It slowly grows over time. I promise that I know. Been there, done that. It is a long, slow road back to restoring your friendships.

Financially, I feel blessed. I have been given much more than most single parents left in my circumstances. Statistics are frightening for widows. In a study on aging from the US Administration entitled "Meeting the Needs of Older Women: A Diverse and Growing Population", almost three quarters of older persons with incomes below the poverty level are women. More than half of elderly widows now living in poverty were not poor before the death of their husbands. Facts show over and over again that women live longer than men and women outlive their savings. It is time to make a change! I still have the time to create more wealth for myself, and, hopefully, you do to. This book will help you create an action plan designed to meet your specific needs.

4. What would you like to change from this point forth?

I would like to be able to eliminate my use of credit cards. About a year ago, I took Dave Ramsey's Financial Peace University course. Some financial advisors cringe at his name, but the course was helpful. Using cash only and a strict budget eliminates compulsive spending. I felt a new confidence when I kept my spending in line with my budget. This fact may seem totally contrary. Often, we think a strict budget will make us feel restricted, but it does the opposite. It gives you confidence and courage that you are gaining maturity. You won't overspend. You also will gain a new peace by feeling in control. You will soon realize that you are in charge of your money, instead of feeling that your money and fears about your money are governing you. Don't let debt imprison you. There is a way out.

So now what?

You have some tough choices ahead. Mass Mutual designed a wonderful seminar called "Pearls of Wisdom." In that talk, one learns that 85% of women wait to do financial planning until a crisis occurs in their life, like death or divorce. Unfortunately, by then it is usually too late. After divorce or death, a woman's standard of living usually drops 23% while a man's standard of living actually goes up by 10%. That's a little frightening, isn't it? I guess his shoe budget drops substantially, but that is not a good enough reason for this discrepancy.

Women, it is time to take charge! Whether you like it or not, 90% of women will be solely responsible for their finances at some point in their lives, so we can't ignore money any longer. It can be a powerful force for good, if we learn to use it wisely.

It is okay if you don't feel totally confident about your money yet. Do we still date even when we are not confident about what we are looking for, or that this person is "the one"? Yes, of course. Through trial and error, we grow and learn. That is the same with managing our money. I don't expect you to have all the answers and I would not dare to say I have all the answers to every person's individual story. What I can offer is a roadmap with pointers on what to beware of with "slick financial advisors" and with important aspects to consider when creating a financial plan.

When my husband passed on, I really had to quickly educate myself about money management and estate planning. First, some friends and I spent endless hours searching for my husband's Will, but we never found it. (We will discuss further the importance of Wills and Trusts in the chapter "Having the Tough Conversation.") This huge problem could have been easily avoided with communication. Renting a safe deposit box in a bank or buying a safe to hold important financial documents would have been an easy solution. This small step would have saved needless legal expenses, and the money could have been used for unexpected demands like burial expenses.

Again, you may ask why there were legal expenses. Doesn't everything automatically go to the wife? Here is where a financial plan makes a difference. My husband never listed me as a beneficiary on his bank accounts. This may seem like a small detail when opening an account, but at some point in life it could be <u>very</u> significant. My husband passed on in Arizona. It was over seven weeks before we got his death certificate. I could not touch any of his accounts without that legal document. If I had not had my own bank account, I would have been in serious trouble.

Let me back up to say that my husband was not a stupid man. He was a lawyer and graduated from UNC Chapel Hill Law School. Over and over, I have heard that lawyers are often notorious for not writing their own Wills and taking care of their estates. Many wives of lawyers have had their homes foreclosed and lost everything because their assets were stuck in probate. Because they had no bank account or credit card in their own name, they lost everything.

I tell my clients over and over again that creating a financial plan is the most loving thing you can do for your family. It will save much heartache. The one thing I wish I could change about the past was my last conversation with my husband in person before he died. My husband and I had never discussed his final wishes. The people at hospice confronted me about my husband's last wishes. I was totally caught off guard. In our final conversation, I had to ask him horrible questions like "Do you want to be cremated? Do you want a service?" I wish I could tell my kids that their dad and I had this amazing final conversation where he told me to love and protect them and make sure they always reached their goals and made new ones, but that wouldn't be the truth. If this book only touches one life and changes one final conversation for another family, I will feel I have accomplished my goal.

The most difficult experience of my husband's passing came a few days later. I had paid the funeral home for my husband's final expenses and was calling them to go over the details of his ashes. He had requested to be cremated. His family, without asking me or offering to pay any of the expense, took his ashes and spread them without including me or my children. I can't imagine a more hurtful act. Again, this painful experience could have been avoided with a legal document stating where and how he would like his ashes distributed.

We get so busy in life rushing around that we put off doing Wills and estate planning, thinking we have so much more time ahead of us, but I want to tell you again that you never know when the unexpected will occur. Love yourself and your family enough to take the time to create a financial plan.

Here is a new question for you . . . do you know how much it costs to be cremated? Well, I had no background or experience in it. I never took a college class in writing an obituary or managing burial expenses. The funny thing is I don't think I am alone. The hospice nurse pulled me aside and said that cremation ranges in cost from $600.00 to $2300. What would I like to do? Again, not being an expert and not wanting to sound like a cheap skate, I asked, "Is there a reason I should choose the $2300.00 one versus the $600.00 one?" The nurse then finally offered some guidance and said that she thought I would be okay with the $600.00 option. It was still a loving choice. Now, let me make this clear that this occurred five years ago so the prices are probably higher now. Have you set aside money for burial expenses? I won't get into more detail, but cremation is by far the cheapest option. You really need to consider how you are going to afford expensive caskets, if that is important to you. I have heard of people going way overboard spending $20,000 to $50,000 on a casket because they want to show their love and respect for their husband. They couldn't afford it, but thought it would have been his dying wish. Many men have voiced almost the other extreme saying, "I am dead. Just put me in a box. Who cares?"

It may sound funny, but isn't it the same with wedding rings? Men go into debt paying for these huge diamond rings for women. If they were both really wise financially they would know to buy a less showy ring and invest the rest. That small bit of extra cash, when left untouched, will accumulate over time to be worth much more than a diamond ring. Currently, the values of diamonds are decreasing instead of increasing, so the ring could steadily lose value over time.

I think it also shows your priorities. Is a big fancy ring what makes you happy? I hope not. Each of us has to learn that material pleasures and endless shopping are not the answer to life's problems. The temporary bliss or shopping high will be erased when you open your next credit card statement.

One of my favorite books is entitled, "The Millionaire Woman Next Door" by Thomas J Stanley, Ph. D. It is such an eye-opener! Most women millionaires are first generation millionaires. They did not come from a wealthy family or marry a rich husband. Instead, they used persistence and determination to reach their goals. Next, the largest number of women millionaires are educators. What does that mean? You don't have to earn a huge salary to be wealthy. Instead, you have to learn to live frugally and within your means. Lastly, none of the women millionaires in the study finished at the top of their classes or believed they were especially smart. This fact comforts me because it shows that being wealthy is not determined solely by who is the smartest or who chooses the smartest investment option. A lot of thought, discipline, genuine relationships and a little bit of luck constitute the recipe for true success.

When looking for the right person or right investment strategy, no one has infinite amounts of time to do research. (It does shock me, though, how much time people consume with online dating.) Each of us must formulate a plan. Before you can find the "right" guy, you need to formulate a list of what qualities are important for you. What are your must haves and what are the things you can live without? I keep my list in a notebook I carry around daily. This list is essential, because it helps us narrow our focus and be more specific about where we can search for the "one". If I don't want a man who drinks, then I shouldn't be going to a bar to find someone. I may do better going to a singles event at a church, or volunteering with a charity organization. Let's learn to use our time wisely and effectively.

Before writing this book, I decided for ten days to do the online dating thing as an experiment. It was definitely comical. I will share many more stories of this experience throughout the book. I met this one guy who spends an hour and a half every night trying to read all the new profiles of women and sending out about five emails each night. He said that if he was lucky, he might get one reply a day or a 20% return on investment. (That might look like a dream in the stock market, but in the stock market, you have to first research deeply to learn more.) Then, he told me he had never been past a first date with any of the girls he met online. I wrote him an email that was brutally honest. It said, "Insanity is doing the same thing over and over again and expecting different results." In a loving way, I told him he was a beautiful person on the inside, but he might want to take an hour each night and go to the gym and workout. Then if he gets back to the online dating in a few months, he might have different results.

The strategy is the same with money. There are infinite possibilities for achieving true wealth. Unfortunately, there is only a finite amount of time to make money and save money. Our financial objectives need to be clearly stated and in proper order. Sometimes we put them in the wrong order because of misinformation. Many parents often make the mistake of putting college planning for their children at the top of their priority list rather than planning for their own retirement. This can create a long-term problem. During their prime money making years, parents are putting away money for college. Yet, children can get loans and often learn valuable lessons having to work their way through college. Paying off credit cards and saving for retirement should be the parents' top concern. Many retirees lack money during their retirement years. They did not plan effectively. People are living longer, so now many people can be retired for as many years as when they were employed.

Let's pause now and create in the space below a list of your priorities in life.

Top Five Financial Goals

1.

2.

3.

4.

5.

Congratulations! By writing down your goals, you have completed a task that only 3% of Harvard Business School MBA graduates have accomplished. In an interesting study conducted in 1979, we learned that only 3% of Harvard MBA graduates had written goals, 13% had goals but never wrote them down, and 84% had no specific goals. Unbelievable! The fascinating part occurred when they interviewed them again 10 years later. The 13% with goals were earning almost twice as much as the 84% with no goals, while the 3% with clear written goals were earning ten times as much as the other 97% put together. Don't take for granted the power of having a firm goal and direction in life.

There are many financial topics still to be discussed, but I hope you have added preparing a Will, discussing final wishes with loved ones, and completing this book to your top five. By the end of the book, you may also add issues like creating an emergency fund (if you don't have one already), eliminating credit card debt, checking your FICO score and creating a budget so you know your monthly and yearly expenses. Did you know that you may have 40% or more of your income going to some form of taxes, which is more than the average family spends on food, clothing and housing?" That number is only going to get worse as the recession continues or if you live in the state of California. Being prepared and working with a financial advisor can save you money instead of cost you money if you find the right one who is honest, ethical and develops a comprehensive plan. This action leads into my next chapter . . .

Ten Common Money Mistakes Women Make

1. **Impulse Buying**

   Never spend more than $50 without waiting 24 hours to consider whether this purchase is essential. (Make sure to check your bank balance too!)

2. **Avoiding the Truth**

   How is it that we can be so organized in all other aspects of our life and have our finances be a mess? Money creates true wealth—emotionally and financially. Let's get in balance.

3. **Using credit cards not cash**

   Credit cards seem a lot less painful and make it easier to avoid the reality of debt. Stop now! Dave Ramsey states that the average ticket at McDonald's went from $4.75 when cash alone was accepted to $7 when credit cards were allowed.

4. **Not tracking daily expenses**

   Have a cute money journal and track all your expenses for at least one month, including your Starbuck's coffee and bottled waters. It will be a wake up call to see how much of your budget is spent on food and eating out.

5. **<u>Buying a new outfit for our next BIG date or event</u>**

This has been a great wake up call. Now I borrow clothes from friends if I need something special. Also, I remember the story my guy friend told about how he canceled on a date with a girl because he knew it was not going anywhere. She turned ballistic because she had bought a new dress just for the event. No man is worth going in debt over!

6. **<u>Not selling old clothes or furniture</u>**

Styles change. We all know that, but you should not just Goodwill everything. You can make money selling things at a consignment store or on Craig's List.

7. **<u>Knock offs usually look just as good as the real thing</u>**

Just think of how many friends have shoes that look amazing and you found out they bought them for $20 at TJ Maxx. You would never know!

8. <u>**Leaving out non-essentials, such as gifts, from the budget.**</u>

Christmas and birthday gifts can be a large budget item that can easily add up unexpectedly. Learn how to use credit card points to buy gifts or create cheap alternatives like candles with a note about how their "light" inspires you.

9. <u>**Books and learning are essential**</u>

Heading to the library and not the bookstore can save you a lot of money.

10. <u>**Get an accountability partner to keep you on track!**</u>

2

If It Looks too Good to Be True . . . It Probably Is!

"So many of us define ourselves by what we
have, what we wear, what kind of house we live
in, and what kind of car we drive . . . if you think
of yourself as the woman in the Cartier watch
and the Hermes scarf, a house fire will destroy
not only your possessions but your self."

- Linda Henley

Doesn't it always seem that the cutest guys are either gay or married? Please explain to me why so many married men feel it is okay not to wear a wedding ring? I don't get it! Wives, please require your husbands to wear rings, or else it should be okay for women to walk around without our rings, too. Then men might get a taste of their own medicine! Some cute guy will come up and start talking to me, and we will have a great conversation. I glance down and see no ring? "Cool," I think to myself, and then maybe half an hour later, he <u>finally</u> mentions his wife. "Hello. Could he have said something earlier?"

Credit card companies can be just as deceiving! I don't know which thought is scarier—all the drunk men on college campuses trying to lure innocent women for one night of pleasure, or all the credit card companies waiting to prey on students who are away from home for their first time, with the promise of independence and easy access to cash. Usually a free pizza, Frisbee, or neon beer cooler is attached with the offer. These salespeople are no fools! Acting like friends, they share beer jokes and college tales with the students, while selling them the ultimate weapon of mass destruction—their first credit card.

Statistics have shown people will do *ANYTHING* not to let go of their first credit card. They feel an immense loyalty that is **NOT** natural. Their relationship with their first credit card will often last longer than most peoples' marriages.

Where does the truth lie? "More young people filed for bankruptcy than graduated from college last year," Dave Ramsey tells individuals during his course, "Financial Peace University." More young people quit college for financial reasons than for educational reasons last year. These statistics need to wake up our country! Giving a teenager a credit card in order to learn how to be responsible with money doesn't work. You must educate them.

Some of you may be single. You are wondering how this relates to you. The facts are still the same. Credit cards lead to excess and indulgence instead of control and moderation. As mentioned before, a perfect example is McDonald's. Before these restaurants accepted credit cards, the average ticket price was $4.75. Now that they accept credit cards, the average ticket price is $7. Cash is king! Using it is the only way to teach or control sticking to a budget. Even if a person pays off his credit cards each month, Dun and Bradstreet research has proven that people spend an additional 12-18% when they use plastic, as compared to cash.

My co-worker told me her latest credit card saga at lunch the other day. She didn't really need another credit card, but she found an offer in the mail that promised 0% interest for life. She and her husband discussed it and couldn't resist. Sound familiar? Within two weeks of the card being delivered, a new letter arrived that said her new interest rate was 21%. It was all a scam! Do you know that invitations for another credit card were accepted by over 18 million people last year? Who really needs another credit card? The sad thing is that they get burned either way. If they cancel the credit card, it hurts their credit score, but if they keep it, it can hurt them with 21% interest.

The gross revenue of credit card companies last year was 150 billion dollars. That is more than the gross revenue of India and Egypt combined! Our wasteful spending must stop! How do we stop this destructive cycle? We stop it by taking back control, learning self-control, setting new goals, and educating our children about how to be responsible with money. Kids see your example. Either adults become role-models of self-control, or this cycle of self-destruction will continue for generations. Get your children involved in the process. When I took Dave Ramsey's Financial Peace University, my kids sat in on the sessions. Dave Ramsey had the helpful idea of getting three containers for each child—one for spending, one for saving and one for giving. Children need to learn they can't just spend all the money they earn. If a child earns $5.00 a week, they should be taught to divide the money—$1.00 goes into giving for church, $2.00 into spending and $2.00 into saving.

Right now, you may be feeling overwhelmed. How do I even start creating a budget? At the start of the Financial Peace University class, half of the students did not know how to make a budget or how to live within a budget. They are not alone. Today, 90% of investors have no financial plan and 60% of workers have saved less than $10,000. It's no wonder our country got into such a big recession. The majority of the population has had no accountability; they have lived for the moment, instead of planning for the future.

Discipline. We, as parents, try hard to instill it in our children. Why are we such contradictions? We can't expect our children to be disciplined in life if we don't guide them in making wise choices with money and relationships. Hopefully, I can save my children some of the growing pains I have experienced. If not, I can at least teach them that the most painful lessons can also be the most valuable ones.

Okay, it's self-examination time again. Go get your wallet and count:

How many credit cards do you have?

Do you know the interest rate on each?

How much credit card debt do you have?

Have you created a timeline for when you will pay it off?

How often do you use your credit card?

What was your largest purchase with a credit card?

When you are in a store, how do you decide what to buy?

Could you stop using your credit cards today and only use cash?

The answers to these questions are fundamental to your financial future. Your credit card spending and debt ratio, including mortgage, are the main factors determining your FICO or credit score. Having a good FICO score is essential. Your interest rates for anything you purchase or credit card you use, are determined by your FICO score. If you have a high FICO score, banks and businesses are willing to offer you a lower interest rate because they know you are responsible and pay your bills on time. If you have a lower score, you will pay higher interest for every credit card, car loan or mortgage you have. FICO scores range from 300 to 850. Your goal is to be between 760 and 850. The scariest part about your FICO score is that there are three different credit bureaus: Equifax, Experian and TransUnion. Each can rank your score differently. Banks use your lowest score, not your highest, when determining your mortgage rate, so beware!

Now, you must stop and take the time to find your credit score. I think you will be shocked. You can get one free annual credit score by going to freecreditscore.gov or by calling 877-322-8228. When I checked, I was surprised. My credit score was lower than I expected because my spending limits on my credit cards were very high. I never imagined this would be an issue. Also, I had a few open credit cards that I had not used for years. I immediately called my credit card companies and lowered my spending limits, renegotiated interest rates, and canceled the unused cards.

How can you improve your credit score? Educate yourself. The first 65% of your credit score is based on two different factors:

1. Do you pay your bills on time?
2. How much debt do you have?

The next three factors that create the last 35% of your score are how long have you had credit cards? Have you applied for new credit cards lately? What is your ratio of credit? Is it credit cards or car loans or student loans or a mortgage?

You may be shocked that there can be well over 1 to 2 points percentage difference on mortgages based on your credit score. I may get offered a fixed rate of 4% for 30 years, while someone with a lower score could easily be offered 5.5 to 6%. Over 30 years that adds up to a lot of extra wealth.

You can't ignore any aspect of your financial picture because all the parts are added up to form your "Circle of Wealth."©

Right now, you may be thinking it would be impossible to ever envision your life without credit card debt, car loans and a mortgage. I was surprised to read that the Census Bureau's American Housing Study recently reported that 76 million households own a home in the United States and of the 76 million, 25 million own their home **free-and-clear of debt**. Wow! One-third of Americans have no mortgage. That number is much larger than I imagined. That means it is much more than just celebrities or the super rich, who own their homes free and clear.

Now, when you are on a date how can you know if your date is responsible with his or her money? **Look at their past!** You may choose to ignore the warning signs, but past behavior is usually the best predictor of the future.

Okay, so now you get to hear the story of my Porsche man . . . How could I have fallen for him? Haven't we all been told <u>not</u> to date a guy who drives a Porsche? The signs are all there. He is driving a showy car, which is never a good choice. He has to find fulfillment in a flashy car, because he doesn't have it within himself. Did you know that the car Thomas Stanley, Ph. D, teaches us most millionaire men drive is a Toyota Camry? They know the car is reliable, safe and comfortable without being precocious. Yet, my friend was smooth and slick. I fell hard and fast. The promise of companionship and a need for speed were irresistible. Whether we want to admit it or not, at some point we are all vulnerable to the promise of instant gratification.

The scary thing is that I completely avoided the warning signs. One of my secret tricks, which I guess won't be secret anymore, is I always bring cash on a date. When the check comes, I may offer to pay the tip. I tell him that I don't use credit cards only cash. Watch his face, and you will learn a lot. I then discuss the Dave Ramsey course. Within a few minutes, he usually tells me how much credit card debt he has. When in his car, I may discuss that I bought a car recently, and then we discuss whether he got a good car loan or paid cash. I quickly learn how financially savvy he is. Is it important for him to fight for a good bargain or does he think money grows on trees?

Please walk into a relationship with your eyes wide open, financially at least. In my heart, I knew my relationship with the Porsche man would never last. He had enormous credit card debt, and we were eating dinner at one of the fanciest restaurants in town. The funny thing was that during dinner, I just wished we were at a casual place. I didn't need a five-course meal. During dinner, he admitted he actually leased his car because he couldn't afford one, and that he was only renting his condo while everyone else in the building owned theirs. These are all red flags—Run!

Needless to say, we never saw each other after that night. It is scary how chemistry can blind you. Please beware. If someone near and dear to you is trying to control your money or is making stupid financial decisions, don't stay around and try to change them. You never will!

I had to laugh, because the last day I was doing the online dating thing, I got an email from a man with a picture of him and his Porsche. I wanted to test if my theory was true. He wrote me a long email about how he thought we were the perfect match because I stated I liked "non-traditional" dates like go-cart racing, playing golf or going for a bike ride. After reading his letter, I checked out his profile. I had to do a double-take when I saw his dating status. He was married!!! Now my curiosity was peaked. Was this guy for real? Yes, he clearly stated he was married, but he and his wife had lost their flame. He would be willing to leave his wife if he could find the "perfect" girl. Wow! I am amazed that there are people out there like that. I know I shouldn't be. Delete.

Today, I ask you to take a small step toward claiming your independence. Please open one credit card in your name ONLY. Don't allow anyone else to have their name on it or use that card. Why? It is your protection. You must establish your own credit score. You may be in the perfect relationship or marriage now, but things can change overnight. A man can leave you, or die, when you least expect it. There are many different outcomes, but in a blink of an eye you can be left alone struggling to find your way. Could you rent an apartment or buy a home? Not without a FICO score. Every individual, single or married, must keep a bank account and credit card in his or her own name to survive! This is no joke. Time and again, I have heard a story where a woman has no credit or money to her name because she and her husband shared bank accounts. Again, the man was no fool. He walked to the bank after he walked out on her, and cleared out everything before she could do any thing, or he racked up an enormous credit card bill that was in both their names so she would be responsible for paying it off. This one joint credit card could force her into bankruptcy and ruin her financial future for at least seven years.

Do I think all men are slime? Of course not! I just want people to be smart and alert. There are ways to protect yourself such as staying away from joint credit cards or bank accounts. These are individual choices, of course; but I am showing you problems that can be avoided by never going down a dangerous path.

Your job is to open only one credit card, just make one or two small purchases on it a month, and make sure you pay your bill <u>on time</u>! Then you will be prepared. Did you know that an employer can look at your FICO score without your permission? It can keep you from getting a job, especially in the financial industry. Potential employers may do a thorough background check on how you manage your money.

> This story has been told to me too many times to ignore. Many widow women, usually between age 65 and 80, try to come into a bank and open their first credit card. Until now, their credit card was in their husband's name. It is very hard for a woman to open a credit card at that age if she has no credit record or job. Please make sure your mothers and grand mothers have a credit card in their name.
>
> THANKS!

Before we move on, I want to tell you one last step I've taken for peace of mind. I have put on a credit freeze with all three credit bureaus. This may seem like a time consuming process, but it is nothing compared to the time it would take to restore your identity, if you became a victim of identity theft.

What does that mean? I put a freeze on my accounts so no one can open a credit card, get a loan or use my personal information in a financially damaging way without my consent. Now, this step can be too difficult for people who are constantly getting loans because you have to freeze and unfreeze your account every time you need to get a new credit card or loan, but I try never to do that. I try to live by the philosophy that if you can't pay cash for it, then don't buy it. I have learned a lot lately about being a more aggressive bargainer, and I use the dollar store regularly without shame.

There is enough information out there on identity theft to scare you to death. We can't live our lives in constant fear, but we can take practical steps to try to limit our liability and make it much harder to be a target. Please take the time to protect yourself. In the case of identity theft, you again lose **all** your control. Often, people spend years and thousands of dollars, including endless hours of lost wages and peace of mind, to try to argue and reestablish their identity and their financial records. I don't want any woman to be a victim. Take the time to be in control.

The opening and closing of credit cards is something we did not discuss in detail earlier. I have often heard people say, "Don't worry. I just opened this store credit card to get the discount today, but I will close it after I pay the bill." Even if they are disciplined enough to remember to close the account at the end of a month, this is a mistake. Steadily opening and closing credit cards will hurt your credit score, too. Remember, when using a credit card, you generally spend between 12-18% more than you would if you paid with cash.

Another common argument I hear for the use of credit cards is, "My card is great. I get airplane miles; so it is really helpful, and ends up saving me money." One I often used was, "My credit card company gives me rewards. I pay for all my Christmas presents with the rewards I get at the end of the year." No free gifts or airline miles are going to get you on the road to financial freedom. It is time to cut those cards up and start changing your lifestyle. You will also have to stay on top of the news because there is talk of credit card companies charging fees to people who pay off their credit cards every month. Get it? They only want you as a customer if they can make money off of you.

While writing this book, I have retreated to a hidden cabin in the Black Mountains of North Carolina. It is an amazing oasis. There is no cell phone coverage or internet access. All that I have is a small television that only plays a few channels. I have been completely astonished at how many courtroom shows there are in the middle of the day. (I work days so I never get to see television during the day.) I think there are around nine or ten different courtroom shows within just a three or four hour period. These are all small court situations where someone believes another person is out to get them or has done them wrong in the past. It shows me that people don't want to be held accountable for their own actions, but they always want to blame someone else for the bad things in their life. Our society has forgotten how to take responsibility and be accountable for our actions.

Our government has been a horrible role model. Our country is in debt over 12 trillion dollars, if you look at the US National Debt Clock. Each day our country goes into debt by another 3.98 billion dollars! We are going to have to be prepared for the consequences. Numbers don't lie. These statistics are old and don't include all the newly unemployed people and those receiving social security. The Social Security Administration projects that the program will pay out more than it takes in by 2018 and by 2042, benefits may run out altogether. I think we can all realize that that timeline may be shorter than we think.

The best action you can take right now to secure a sound financial future is to get rid of all your debt. Start with credit cards. They usually have the highest interest rates. Then move on to student loans and car loans that can be almost as burdensome. You should have made a list of your credit cards earlier in this chapter. Slowly, eliminate all but one or two. Pick the card with the highest interest rate and put all the extra money you have into paying it off first. Just don't forget to pay the minimum balance on the others to keep your credit score stable. This action will take discipline, and you will have to learn to say "no", not only to yourself, but to friends and family. You may get teased for being a cheapskate, but that is okay. I would rather be a cheapskate who will have a retirement savings versus someone who lives a fancy lifestyle with no savings at all. On CNN television this morning, the announcer stated that in the

United States, 43% of the population has not saved more than $10,000. That amount of money won't last very long in the case of a medical emergency, or if your house burns down. Please remember that "Saving money saves lives." It can save yours. Start today!

The biggest lesson I have learned in financial planning is that nothing is what it appears to be from the outside. You may have a friend who lives in the biggest house with the most amazing shoe collection in town, but then you learn secretly that her husband is going to prison because he cooked the books for an organization. Never trust the surface picture.

This spring my favorite show was a new reality show on Bravo called, "The Millionaire Matchmaker." It made me laugh and put life in proper perspective. In my favorite episode the director called her client "white trash", but he was worth over 100 million dollars. He invited a woman on his private jet down to his "compound" in Miami. As soon as they got on his private plane, he started offering her junk food and said that candy bars were his favorite food. When they arrived at his house, he offered her something to eat. The audience assumed it would be a very elegant dinner because in previous episodes, the millionaire had rented out a restaurant or brought in a private chef for an exquisite dinner. He goes into his freezer and grabs her frozen potato skins and offers them to her for dinner. From there, the date only got worse because they went to his private driving range to hit golf balls. He suddenly realized he had to go to the bathroom and doesn't want to walk all the way back to the house. Instead, he relieves himself in a bush right near her. Need I go on? Some of your bad dates don't look so bad anymore do they? No amount of money was going to teach this man class, etiquette or how to respect women. Marrying a sugar daddy or someone really rich does not guarantee happiness or success.

A wonderful example of realizing how costly a dream could be was stated clearly by Patrick Kelly in his book "Tax-Free Retirement." A man had always dreamed of owning a boat and kept thinking of all the wonderful family memories that could be created on that boat. Finally, the man found his dream boat and took out a loan to purchase it. The boat had a sticker price of $43,000. Unfortunately, the boat would cost much more when you started adding insurance, fuel, maintenance, taxes and storage fees. If John had taken the money and invested it wisely for twenty-five years, that $43,000 could have grown to over 3 million dollars. Wow! Are you willing to sacrifice all that long-term growth for the immediate satisfaction of a few weekends out on the lake? With the right knowledge, you have the power to make wise choices. Use this same example when considering buying your next car or planning your next trip. My dear friends bought an amazing boat and used it all the time their first summer. Unfortunately, work and kids' sports became so demanding that they only took it out once last summer.

We must learn to gain control of our finances. Doing this we can learn to recognize the qualities we want in others who are also responsible and smart with their investing and relationships. I think you will quickly see that they often go hand in hand. The next chapter will help you see the warning signs of people who want to control you and your money. Keep reading . . .

3

Getting Rid of the Blame Game

"This is the year of no excuses!"

- Theresa Salihu-Musso,

Results Unlimited

How often have we beaten ourselves up over a broken relationship? We like to replay every event in our head to see if there is anything we could have done differently to change the outcome. I am guilty of endless hours of self-pity over broken relationships and wondering if I will ever find the "perfect" guy. Why does it look so easy for others to find the "one", but it seems so hard for me? When I am about to give up, I usually hear the phone ring. I will never figure out how my friends know to reach out to me at my lowest moments. They give me the pep talk I need to keep going and impersonalize it.

Before we go any further in this book, I think it is really important to again emphasize how "our attitude determines our altitude." Surrounding ourselves with people who build us up will help keep us moving forward. Remember, you often take on the characteristics of the people you surround yourself with.

Women know the value of friendship. We need other women to share our feelings and be a sounding board for different activities. These friendships are powerful forces for good.

Recently, I have found an "accountability" partner. This is someone I check in with at least once a week. We each sit down and see if we achieved the goals we set for ourselves the past week. Then we create new goals for the upcoming week. In this environment, we learn that excuses are not accepted. It has been so important in helping me to move forward and stay on track. Please find someone to be your "accountability" partner. You can start by just meeting for lunch or coffee once a week. This small step will keep you energized and motivated.

During a leadership training session, Russ McCarter, Ph. D., a personal coach, taught me to **not** stay in BED all day. He said that bed stands for:

Blame

Excuses

Denial.

Instead we needed to take control with our OAR. OAR stands for:

Ownership

Accountability

Responsibility.

Remember it is our own thinking that determines our wealth. We are as wealthy as we believe we should be. Think about it . . . we each decide how we are going to react to situations. We can decide to face challenges from a victim mentality with a "Why me?" thought or decide to not dwell on the past. Instead, we should look at each setback as an opportunity to learn and we will become a Victor. No one who is truly successful made it without climbing many mountains, and failing sometimes.

These failures often gave successful people the drive to never quit and always keep working to achieve more.

One of the most touching things I have read recently is in a book called "The One Minute Millionaire" by Robert Allen and Mark Victor Hansen. In a section entitled "Extraordinary Dream Teams", they share the story of how Thomas Edison's New Jersey laboratory burned to the ground. The next morning, his friend Henry Ford arrived with a check for $750,000 and told him to "start building again." Ford would not allow any interest to be paid on his loan. He sincerely believed in his friend and just wanted to encourage him to persevere and rebuild. That illustrates someone I want on my team! Imagine how much that check that Henry Ford wrote would be worth in present day terms. Henry Ford truly knew that money was not how you judge wealth. It is by character, determination and resilience.

What is often the difference between people who achieve great things and others who keep doing the same thing every day? I think it is one's vision! My accountability partner and I now do a blog talk radio program once a week. Please come listen at www.blogtalkradio.com and search for datingourmoney.

In a past episode, we discussed Five Steps to Achievable Goals. These are important:

1. **Determine what you really want.**

2. **Write down your goals!**

3. **Visualize achieving your goals.**

4. **Work back from the goal and create baby steps today that get you started.**

5. **Go and do it! Take action NOW!**

Five Steps to Achievable Goals

Step One: Determine What You Really Want

Some people may believe that goal number one is too simplistic. Yet, it is also very complicated. I often hear many friends say they want to get married. This is so important to them. Yet, my married friends often comment on how they are jealous of my lifestyle because I have a freedom that they don't have right now. I only answer to myself. At night, I can stay

45

up late working while they feel a responsibility to spend time with their husbands. Neither choice in life is good or bad. I miss having a person to take out my trash and be my sounding board, while my married friends have that support system. One just needs to make sure they go into any situation with their eyes wide open, knowing the consequences of their decisions.

Step Two: Write down your goals!

This should be easy to understand after reading about the Harvard MBA study. Yet, I want to make sure you go one step further. After writing these goals, please hang them in a place you see daily. One of my dear friends has them posted on her refrigerator door. I usually keep mine on the bathroom mirror. It is so important that we don't lose sight of our vision!

Step Three: Visualize Achieving Your Goals

Completing this book has been a mighty task. When I believe I will finally have a moment to work, the school calls saying I have to pick up a child because he got hurt or some other unexpected crisis occurs. To finish all the editing, I had to imagine what it would be like to tell everyone I completed the book and thus to get past that last hump. Some people create an affirmative statement that they repeat daily saying that they have already completed their goal. This is one way of self-motivation. I have also cut out pictures to display on the front of my journal that keep me focused on my higher goal—helping other women!

Step Four: Work back from the goal and create baby steps today that get you started.

I have been training for a mini-triathlon while writing this book. Learning how to swim again has definitely been the toughest part of my training. I never have been a big swimmer nor did I swim on a team growing up. Just the thought of swimming 10 laps non-stop seemed overwhelming. Then I started to break down the swimming into small baby steps. First I started swimming two laps, then four laps, and more. Each week I now have a goal of swimming five more laps than the week before. I am way beyond what I needed for the race but now swimming laps has become a test of endurance and a mental victory for me. I love it! Having met my goal in swimming has given me the confidence that I can handle other challenges in my personal or professional life, also. It is important to have one aspect of your life where you take time for yourself.

Step Five: Go and do it! Take action NOW!

Talk is cheap, so let's just do what we need to get done. Sometimes the only way you can learn is through trial and error. As a mother, I feel that way all the time. I can preach and preach to my kids to remember to bring their sports equipment or their violin to school. Unfortunately, they don't change their inaction practices until they have to sit out of an activity. Then they finally learn.

You can talk and talk to people about dating, but nothing fully prepares you for going on your first date again after being widowed. You just have to do it. It can seem painful, but you survive. Slowly, you learn that life will go on and maybe someday you will find love again.

Right now, the action I want you to take is turning the page. There is so much more for us to learn together!

4

Take the Time!

"You don't just luck into things . . .
You build step by step, whether it's
friendships or opportunities."

- Barbara Bush

One of the things that has shocked me the most when getting
back into the dating world is men's attitude when I don't drink
on a date. It has been a real eye opener and reality check. The
first time I was on a date when a man got offended that I didn't
drink, our kids were around. I was shocked because I would
never drink around my kids and know many friends who have
made it their rule that they will drink, but not around their kids.

How can you tell your kids not to drink and then be drinking in front of them? Now I know this example may seem very extreme to many people because most people drink. However, it has become one of my gold standard tests. I have now seen how differently men confront this issue. The men who get mad are mad because they realize they aren't going to be able to be in control or be able to dominate me. I know from that moment on there will be no second date. Other men are pleasantly surprised and realize that it shows a great deal of maturity and self-respect not to drink. They even go as far as taking a cue from me and not drink when around me. Ladies, this may shock you but I might try not drinking on first dates. You will learn a lot and also gain a lot more self-confidence.

When I was 16, my parents offered me a contract that I could accept or not accept. It stated that if I didn't drink, smoke or do drugs, then I would receive a specific amount of money. Now, my sister and I decided to accept this contract, but my brother did not. You might be wondering how this relates to financial planning, but it does. How people react to different circumstances and situations teach you a lot about them. I learned quickly in my teenage years who my friends were and who they weren't. The contract became something easy to fall back on at a party when I wasn't drinking. Some stupid guys would usually come up and say, "Oh, come on. Your parents will never know. Just drink one beer" or "That contract is lame. No amount of money is worth not getting drunk over." I knew he didn't respect me, and we had no future. Other people said I became a role model for them, and they loved the idea of the contract. Those people I kept around.

Please remember that I never judged someone if they drank or not, and still don't today. That is each person's decision. All I ask is for people to respect my choice, and I will respect theirs. Time quickly helped me sort through who were my friends in high school and college. I had an amazing group of friends and boyfriends all through high school and college that were important in shaping who I am today. Without alcohol as a crutch, you had to learn an enormous amount of self-confidence, especially dancing on tables when everyone else was drunk. You had to learn not to worry about looking like a fool. You learned how to be happy and laugh at yourself when it was appropriate.

Right now, we are going to talk about the qualities I want you to search for when finding a good man and a good financial planner. You don't want a shark and there are many out there. What do I mean? "Shark" defines a person or financial planner who is in for the quick sale, or a one-night stand. He is slick and he is smooth, but he also lacks patience. Time is the one quality he doesn't understand. As a financial planner, he wants the quick sale, and then he will be out of your life for good. Don't expect him to return calls after he sealed the deal. He is high-pressure and will keep harassing until you give in. RUN!

The secret of recognizing a good man or financial planner is finding the one who takes the time to get to know you. This man or financial planner cares about understanding what makes you tick and what your goals and plans for the future are. However, can he be your cheerleader and push you to reach your full potential?

When meeting with a client, it often takes three or four two-hour meetings before selling a product. A lot of time is spent learning what goals this individual, couple, or business owner has. Financial planners also have to learn a lot about their client's comfort level with investing. It is never wise to offer a client a product that does not put the client's mind at ease when considering the future. They should not lose sleep worrying about their money and retirement. A Financial Planner's goal is the exact opposite—reassurance. We can't give that without taking the time to educate them. The example we use that I think is helpful, is this one:

If I gave you the choice of having a famous golfer's clubs or his skill, which would you choose? Of course, we would all say skill! Tiger Woods could probably go to a garage sale and pick up an old set of clubs and play against any one of us and still put us to shame. His skill is what is so valuable and the clubs are secondary. That is also true of good financial planners. We take the time to educate our clients, because there is so much false information out there. Now, I know you are not all going to come knocking at the door of my business, so I want you to learn what qualities to search for in a good financial planner.

Important questions to ask a financial planner:

How long have you been in the business?

Have you stayed with this company the whole time?

Do you work with a partner?

What does this process involve?

How do you get paid?

What kind of products are you licensed to sell?

How much time will this process take?

What do I need to bring to the first meeting?

How do you do your research about products to offer a client?

How often do we get together to update this information?

Now I will show you what answers to be listening for.

How long have you been in the business?

Okay, I am new in the financial industry compared to many, but I always have my partner Claudia, and often times her husband too, when I meet with clients. Combined, we have over forty years of experience in the industry. There is so much to know in the financial industry that no one can be an expert at everything. You almost have to create a niche to really keep up with all the new laws and changes. In our office, there are people who specifically focus on selling disability insurance or long-term care insurance. (In chapter 6, I will explain all the different types of insurance).

Have you stayed with this company the whole time?

If a financial advisor keeps jumping ship and changing companies, this should be a red flag. I've only switched companies once because of not agreeing with my boss. If people have changed companies a number of times, they are not meeting a quota, which often means that people do not trust them. Secondly, you begin to wonder if all their actions are above board, or if they switch right before they get busted. It takes enormous time and energy for financial planners to develop a client base. You never decide to switch firms easily, because many of your clients may not come along with you.

Do you work with a partner?

Do I need to even say that two heads are better than one? This is obvious. I think a partnering relationship is essential to look for. Why? First, this team is there to truly help others. They know they could possibly get a bigger commission by going it alone, but they also know they can be of more value to the client when information is shared. It creates a wonderful system of checks and balances. Secondly, since my name is on the line with the rules of compliance when I meet with clients and recommend products, I am only going to work with people I absolutely trust and know are ethical.

What does this process involve?

This is so important to find out. Does the financial planner go through a fact-finding process with you to get a picture of your whole financial framework? Developing a financial plan is like building a house. You have to look at many elements, not just one. If someone is only trying to sell you insurance or mutual funds, walk away. Has the prospective financial planner asked if you have a Will or Trust in place? Have you been asked who the beneficiary on your life insurance policy is? These questions identify people you want to talk to because they are after the bigger picture. Only a lawyer can draft a Will or Trust documents. Yet, a financial advisor who cares knows that it is essential to the security of your whole financial picture to have a Will. If you die, the planner needs to be certain that the money is going where you wanted and not where a court decides. He/ she needs to take the time to ask clients who you want to be the guardian of your kids if something happened to you or you and your spouse. A lawyer could ask the same questions, but he will be charging a lofty hourly fee.

Choosing a financial planner is probably one of the most terrifying and important decisions that an individual or couple has to make. Each individual and/or couple must decide who they want to be executor of their estate, guardian of their kids, holder of durable power of attorney and designee for durable power of attorney for healthcare.

How does a financial planner get paid?

This has become one of the hot topics of the financial industry. Many people stress using only a fee-based system. In that instance, the choices recommended by the financial planner depend on the financial planner's evaluation of the circumstances of the client.

In my office, we offer both flat fee-based and commission-based sales. The most important quality to look for in this choice process is honesty. Does your prospective choice tell you that he/she gets paid by commissions from selling different products? If so, will he or she make the best choices for you or select those which produce the largest commissions? I am probably one of the most boringly honest people in the business, because I am going to give my clients the best product for them, no matter what the commission is for me. There are few people like me, but I surround myself with people who share that same philosophy. As a result, I rarely do fee-based planning—only when clients absolutely insist on it—as my commissions usually total less than a fee would come to.

(Please note that I am not trying to sell my financial services, because I have had to put my financial licenses on hold to publish this book. I am only trying to offer an inside perspective learned through working in the industry.)

I went to Davidson College in Charlotte, North Carolina for my first two years of college. This may not mean much to you, but there are only three colleges in the country today that still have a working honor code. That means that the school allows students to take their exams at any time during a one-week period. My roommate may have taken the same Art History exam yesterday that I am taking tomorrow, but no one cheats. People take the honor code seriously, and people are instantly suspended by their own peers if they break any part of the honor code. It is a powerful thing to see, especially in our world where lies seem so rampant. (I better add a quick note that I left the school after two years because it did not have the major I wanted to pursue, not because of any incident.) If I met a graduate of Davidson College or William and Mary College in the financial industry, I would seriously consider working with them, because they understand the value of honesty in themselves and others.

What kind of products are you licensed to sell?

If you ask this question of prospective choices, you learn a lot about their diversity. You learn if they walk the walk, or just talk the talk. I can sell every financial product including stocks, bonds, mutual funds, annuities and any insurance product. Many people in my office have not earned their Series 7 license, so they can only sell insurance. That makes it very hard for them to look at your whole financial picture, because they are not allowed to discuss investments with a client unless they bring another partner into the meeting with them. Doing this would make me nervous because they are totally dependent on the other person's recommendations and don't have the knowledge to add their own opinion.

I won't lie that I worked really hard to get my Series 7 license. Being a single parent, I had to study for months from 10 pm to 2 am in the morning, regularly living on 3-4 hours of sleep because I knew this test was essential to my career and helping people create an effective financial plan for the future. People who work with me know that I take my job seriously and treat each client as a new case. I won't sell them any product that is not designed to meet their personal goals. Making money quick is not the answer. I heard on the radio yesterday a quote that said, "Fame lasts for a moment, but character is developed over a lifetime." I want to always be known as a person of character, who puts my client's interest ahead of my own or any sales quota I am supposed to meet.

What do I need to bring to a first meeting?

Here is another question that helps you quickly recognize a financial planner's motive. If they ask you to bring nothing, then they probably just want to sell you one product to meet their quota and move on to someone else. We email our clients a whole list of items to bring, like a copy of all recent financial statements, their Will and estate planning documents, their last social security statement, and all insurance products they own. This may seem overwhelming for some people, but it helps sort through who is going to take this process seriously. You may be wondering why we ask someone to bring in their social security statement. "I can't find mine", is often the common reply. This statement comes once a year, a month before your birthday and indicates how much you should plan to receive from the government when you retire (if social security still exists.) This helps with retirement planning.

How do you do research on the products you offer your clients?

Ok, I may get in trouble for writing this, but I was shocked when I went in for an interview with a very well known investment company that I had respected for years. I asked the interviewer the question, "How do I know which products to offer my clients? Do we get some training on how to pick specific mutual funds or bonds?" He said that was completely up to me. The only training I received about selecting products was a two week class in New York that helped me more with the fundamentals of selling.

This was a huge wake up call to me. Readers, you are giving financial planners or advisors the money you have worked tirelessly to save. BE CAREFUL! Don't give it to just anyone. Many may not have much more background or experience than you do.

The big problem is that when a planner is new in the industry, he is so busy trying to develop a client base that he may have very little time to study and research all the investment choices out there. That is why you do better to partner with someone who has **years** of experience! Your bosses in the investment firms or insurance industry don't care what product financial planners are selling the client, just that they are actively selling and bringing money into the firm.

How often do planners and clients get back together to update this information?

Listen intently. Check your financial planner's body language. Is he/she starting to squirm, or confidently saying that you'll meet at least once a year, and hopefully more, depending on the changes in tax laws and market volatility.

The Choice

Trust your gut when making your choice. In dating and choosing a financial planner, your gut instinct should be an important consideration. Does this seem natural? Will this person or group of people listen to me? Do you sense he or she is knowledgeable and ethical? Is the planner only thinking about himself or do you think he/she has your best interest at heart?

You don't have to make that decision at that moment. Tell the financial planner you want time to think about it. It should be a very important decision that you don't take lightly. Ask for references so you can contact one or two current clients, if you were not directly referred by a close friend or colleague.

Hopefully, you are not going to sleep with the man on a first date, if you are looking for a long-term commitment. Let's be honest. Sex can add a new element into the relationship that might jade you having a clear vision. I know many people, including myself, who will openly admit that they stayed in a relationship much longer than they should have because the physical attraction was so strong.

I have had to learn from my mistakes. Don't jump into any relationship with a man or with your money unless your eyes are wide open about where this is headed.

Please hire a financial planner if you do not like or have time to create, save, and protect your future. Hiring a planner is essential for designing a financial road map that works for you. I can give you overall advice and guidance, but each situation is unique and each state has radically different laws. In our Will and Estate Planning section, I will tell you some of the strange laws that North Carolina has on intestate property or property distribution when a spouse passes on. You would never believe it!

In our office, I work with mostly single and divorced women. It is really important to update legal documents after a divorce. If you leave your ex-husband as beneficiary of your 401 k plan and you suddenly die, there is no way for your family to get your 401k back. Unfortunately, I have seen someone in the midst of a divorce die and all her property went to her soon to be ex. The family could do nothing about it. It was tragic!

Single parents also need to be very aware of what can happen if they leave their underage children as beneficiaries. Do you really want your child at 18 to receive a huge chunk of money that they can burn through? No. As a result, most people set up a Trust and make a Trust the beneficiary of a life insurance policy. Then the Trust can be designed in numerous ways. Currently, many of our clients have their Trust set up so their children will receive different sums of money when they are 25, 30 and 35. Until then, the Trust advisor manages the money, so it is wisely dispersed and not consumed.

Please stop and take the time to get your finances in order. This book is only the first step in the process. I will try to make myself available to readers to answer questions, but I am still a single mother trying to juggle and balance everything, too.

Don't let the Madoff scandal scare you away from financial planners for good. We have all gone on bad dates but gotten back out there knowing he was just a bad apple. That is the same with Madoff. There are plenty of ethical financial planners who have your best interest at heart. You just have to search for them like you search for a good man!

5

It is Good to Shop Around!

"No one can figure out your worth but you."

- Pearl Bailey

Girls, this is our chapter. No man can ever argue that women don't know how to shop. Many women even amaze me with how they have shopped for the ultimate bargain. They know what they can afford and are ruthless in getting the best deal. Through the internet, women have become very savvy at doing research. They can find the perfect shoes or dress at overstock.com or other popular websites for a third the price of normal retail. Now I want you to use that same energy and passion and towards investing. Then your money will increase so dramatically over time that you can have a closet full of "Jimmy Choo" shoes without a thought. This is due to the power of compounding. We will discuss it in more detail later in this chapter.

How many years does an average woman spend shopping over her lifetime? 8 years! I was stunned to read this answer in <u>Real Simple</u> magazine (November 2010). Think of all the "profitable" things you could have done with eight years of your life. (I believe the statistic is true because I seem to spend way too much time buying groceries for two growing boys!)

Why do we spend so much time talking among ourselves about men and shoes, when we really need to be talking about money? We should be spending the same amount of time on the internet, learning about investing, as we do searching for a stylish new purse.

Money is defined by many as "stored energy." We cannot get our time back, just like we can't get back our money. We earned the money by expending our energy for others. We should care about our money the same way as we care about our children or pets. It is our path to a better future.

Time always seems to be in short supply. It is something we often lack and want more of. Time is a dwindling commodity, like most of our stock portfolios are, with the economic downturn. We thought our money was safe or our financial advisor would keep our retirement from shrinking. Unfortunately, the reality for most has been the exact opposite. I think the last few months have been a wake-up call. No longer can we sit back and expect the stock market to go up and up. Each of us plays a role in protecting our assets. No one will protect your money as well as you.

People are finally realizing they must put a value on each dollar. A few months ago, I remember gas prices spiking outrageously. The gas stations near my house were charging about $.15 to $.25 per gallon more than gas stations five minutes away. This difference quickly adds up with long commutes, or spending a lot of time driving children to their schools and outside activities. Isn't that the same with mutual funds? There are thousands of choices for a growth mutual fund alone. Their returns can vary sharply. How can we know which one to buy? SHOP AROUND and do your research.

This may seem a little basic for some, but I have had many girlfriends come up to me and ask me what a mutual fund is.

For a novice investor, I would always recommend investing in mutual funds while you are learning. A mutual fund is a managed group of individual stocks that share a similar theme.

Here is a perfect example. If I want to buy a perfect cocktail dress for a black tie affair, I have two choices. My first option is to go to a small specialty store that has a few very expensive dresses that I know would be totally unique, or I could go to the mall where I would have more choices and could find a cheaper dress. A single stock is like a dress at the specialty store. The dress can often be pricey and too much for almost any of us to afford, but it definitely offers a unique choice. The mall is like a mutual fund because it takes a number of beautiful dresses and puts them all in one place. One share of a mutual fund involves small holdings in lots of stocks. This makes it a safer investment, and typically it costs less.

With mutual funds, the diversification or combination of many choices together, is what makes them an attractive investment. Your money is grouped with a number of other investors, so the fund managers can buy lots of stocks. You will not be hurt if the value of **one** stock goes down sharply, since most mutual funds do not allow more than 2% of the fund in one stock. Your money is actively managed each day, so the managers will buy and sell in relation to the fluctuations in the market. You can pick a specific area that you would like to focus on, such as international growth. In that case, it would be like going into a mall, knowing you only wanted a red dress and so all you were choosing from were red dresses.

We all know that it is good not to put all our eggs into one basket, just as our moms used to preach. This means it is okay to keep dating other men until you have a commitment from one, just as you would be willing to look at many colors of dresses until you decide on one. You might be shocked to see a purple dress that looks perfect because of its unique design. Having the courage to try something new may be the recipe for success with both money and men.

Financial planners will throw around the words "asset allocation" a lot. This means they want to put your eggs or money in many different baskets to protect you. Financial planners will often recommend that people own between 8 to 10 different mutual funds, so you have a proper "asset allocation." During the recent economic downturn, many people have lost much of their retirement income, because they were too heavily invested in one stock.

Studies have indicated that "over time, more than 90% of an investment portfolio's return is the result of overall asset allocation—the percentage of savings in stocks, bonds and cash—not the particular investments held." (2004 Ibbotson Associates). It is wise to understand what the different forms of allocation are.

Common Categories for Asset Allocation (or diversification):

Growth

Value

Small

Mid-cap

Large Cap

International Growth

International Value

Emerging Markets or Emerging Growth

Bond

Money Market (Cash)

S&P Index

Each of these categories has a definition that can change depending on the judgment of the mutual fund company. On the internet, you can see the specific definition of each at Investopedia.com. I will try to give you a brief overview of each:

Growth funds are usually a more aggressive choice picked especially by younger investors because they can be volatile. They definitely are not as safe as other options, particularly bonds. A growth stock is a company that is experiencing an increase in either its earnings or its sales. This company is expanding and usually has large potential for expansion in the future, but investors could see some highs and lows that come with learning curves. Usually these companies do not pay out dividends, so investors want the price of the stock or fund to rise sharply over time.

Value funds are usually companies that analysts see as "underpriced or undervalued" compared to the fundamental strength of the company and the pricing of similar companies in the same industry. These are companies that currently have lost favor in the eyes of analysts. Usually, they are much safer than growth stocks, because they pay a dividend to investors.

Yet, investors often do not see the same increase in price with these stocks as they do with a growth fund.

Small Cap Funds can definitely vary in definition. Most Small Cap Funds purchase companies with $300 million to $2 billion in "market capitalization." This is calculated by multiplying the number of company shares outstanding by the price per share.

Mid Cap Funds stand for mid-size capitalization companies. They usually range in value from $2 billion to $10 billion.

Large Cap Funds are large capitalization companies. You should have heard of all these companies before, such as General Electric or IBM. They have market capitalizations of more than $10 billion dollars. The Dow Jones Industrial Average is an index made up of 30 large cap stocks.

International Funds focus on buying securities all around the world, so they are not hurt if one part of the world gets in an economic "slump". They may focus on purchasing mostly non-American securities. Most investors like to add some international funds to their portfolios for diversification. In the past, there have definitely been times when funds invested in international markets such as China have done better than funds invested in the US stock market.

Emerging Market Funds focus on buying securities in developing companies that may be relatively unstable economically and politically right now. Yet, they have strong potential as they build a more reliable economy. These stocks have a large potential for future growth, but they are also one of the highest risk investments. Emerging markets include Eastern Europe, Latin America and Middle Eastern countries as examples.

Bond Funds are usually considered one of the safest investments. They are especially recommended for people who are drawing close to retirement. The money is invested with (put on loan to) state and local governments or stable businesses that are judged reliable to repay the debt with interest. (Suze Orman speaks very strongly against bond funds, so please do not think I am completely in favor of them.) I am only laying out the options. For some people they offer safe investments because their returns are generally less volatile. It is often better to buy individual bonds than pay the commission of a bond fund. Under current market conditions, I do not think most bond funds are a wise choice, because returns are low and keeping up with inflation is an issue. I would concur with Suze Orman that utility stocks with high paying dividends are a better and more profitable investment currently.

Money Market Funds are usually a place where people store un-invested money. Some people may call them a "holding tank". The problem is that you do not want to store your money there for very long, because the rate of inflation can outweigh your potential return. Currently, there is a very low return on your money—often less than 1%.

S&P Index Funds are the cheapest way to invest in the market. These funds are "passively" managed, so their fees are much lower. Instead of a manager choosing what securities to buy, these funds mimic the exact stocks found in the S&P index. You can easily invest in other index funds, but these are the most commonly used.

When I started in the financial industry, my brother gave me a wonderful book entitled, "A Random Walk Down Wall Street" By Burton Malkiel. In this book, the author says investing in index funds is the "no-brainer step." Why? In an index fund, there is no fund manager to pick and choose stocks. Instead the index is comprised of the same stocks that the index holds. The S&P 500 is the most well known index. It is made up of 500 major corporations in the United States. Because there is no active fund manager and the fund rarely buys new stocks, their expense fee is substantially lower than that of other funds. In Malkiel's book, he states, "Public index funds can be run at a fee of less than 1/10 of 1 percent. Actively managed public mutual funds charge annual management and market expenses that, on average, are 150 basis points (1 ½ percentage points per year.)" As a result, "Between 1974 and 2006, for example, the S&P 500 outperformed more than three-quarters of the public equity mutual funds. The average annual return for the S&P 500 during this period was more than 1 ½ percentage points better than that of the median fund." Page 360.

Why do I state this? It's because I want you to start taking baby steps with investing. I would never tell a recently divorced woman or widow to go out and just start dating every night of the week. No. I would have her go out one night a week or one night a month, depending on her comfort level. Then she will get back in the game slowly.

Inaction is not the answer. With personal finances, I know the number of choices can seem overwhelming to a woman. We often decide to do nothing because we believe we are not well enough informed. Instead of at least stepping in, we take no action. This mindset is dangerous and must stop! You don't have any more excuses. I am clearly showing you that no one has to be an expert to make money. You can always ask a financial planner for help.

With my first job in the financial industry, I asked my boss how he chose one mutual fund over another. He said, "Don't lose sleep picking one fund over another. As long as you chose a mutual fund in the top ten percent, you should be fine." Information on the top-performing 10% of mutual funds is available to anyone on Morningstar.com.

Every day you are invested you are getting a step closer to your goal of a future without fear. Create a future where you control your money, instead of it controlling you. This doesn't happen overnight, though. If you need $50,000 a year to live today, statistics clearly state that you will need 3 times that amount in 35 years just to maintain your current lifestyle. (That assumes a 3% annual inflation rate.)* Until the recent economic downturn, inflation had been closer to 5%.

When products like Silly Bandz or Crocs first came out, they were trendy and overpriced. Right now, some financial advisors believe the S&P 500 Index is "too popular". At the present investors should look into broader indexes such as the "Russell 3,000, the Dow/Wilshire 5,000 Stock Index, or the MCSI broad U.S. index. If you also want to tap into the international market, there are international index funds to look for, such as the Vanguard International Index Fund.

The last type of index you may hear thrown around is a REIT. This stands for a real estate investment trust, a trust that holds investments in many pieces of real estate. These can be very risky and expensive, but for some investors they are a good compromise.

Now you are going to ask me, "What is the secret ratio for investing? Should you have 40% in bonds and 60% in the stock market or 50% in both?" The answer is simple. There is no universal law that governs everyone. A lot depends on your comfort level with investing. Will you lose sleep if you see your portfolio declines or will you stay calm knowing you have time and the market has always recovered? Historically, investors will do much better if they stay calm and not take their money out with every web and flow. Staying calm when you see a 10% drop in your money may not work for you. Then you need to find some other less volatile products to help diversify your portfolio. This is why financial planners spend so much time learning about peoples' investment philosophy.

Patrick Kelly in his book "Tax-Free Retirement" shows clearly the power of time. His mom use to ask him a simple question. "Patrick, would you rather have someone give you $1,000,000 dollars or one penny that doubled its value every day for a month?" The answer is startling. "That penny is worth almost eleven times that million dollar offer for a 30-day month ($10,737,418.24) or twenty-one and a half times more than the million dollar offer for a 31-day month ($21,474,836.48 to be exact.)

When we take our money out of the market quickly as a reaction to fear, it can often be very harmful. We lose the power of compounding, as we have seen in the example with the penny. No one knows how to "time" the market perfectly, so you can miss out on gains or incur losses trying to enter when the market is going up or exit when it is going down. You are better to keep your money where it is, even in volatile times, unless you need to use it within a year or two for retirement or college or another big capital expense. If you have your mutual fund set to reinvest your dividends (which I encourage), you can buy more shares of stock when the price per share is down. That means when the market goes back up, you will have more shares, which means increased assets!

My partner, Claudia, tells clients very clearly that we wish all financial products had all three of these important qualities: growth, safety, and liquidity (meaning the ability to get your money quickly.) Unfortunately, all investment products are a mixture of only two. Money market accounts offer safety and liquidity but very little growth. (I think the current interest rate of a money market account is less than 1%) That amount of interest won't keep up with inflation, but it is important to have. Your money market account should hold your emergency fund. Everyone needs to have established a 3 to 6 month emergency fund to safe guard you and your family from foreclosure or bankruptcy. Let's face facts. The things we never expect to happen, sometimes happen. Almost all the husbands on my street have been laid off from corporate America, where only a month or two before the wives reassured everyone that their husband's job was safe. There is no more job-security in America anymore. Your emergency fund should be in a money market fund that you never touch. Personally, I have mine with ING Direct which you can sign up online. It offers higher rates of return than standard mutual fund companies or banks.

Mutual funds or stocks offer growth and liquidity because you can sell them quickly, but they don't necessarily offer safety. As we discussed earlier, many elderly couples saw their entire retirement disappear as Washington Mutual Bank went bankrupt, because they had all their retirement in one basket.

The best way to protect yourself is to diversify. No one should have a majority of his/her money in one stock. It is too dangerous. Remember, this money represents all your time and energy. This is what you worked so hard for for so many years. Be smart about it, and don't let anyone pressure you into a decision or invest in some "special" investment instrument. You have a right to look at a number of different financial advisers to see how their views of the market and investing differ, and it takes awhile to find the perfect fit—just like buying a good pair of jeans.

When I did the online dating thing, I was about to give up on men. I had heard so many horrible stories, I was on overload. What shocked me the most online was how many choices I had, and within a few minutes of submitting my profile, my mailbox was full of greetings from men with every imaginable background and job. In my day-to-day life, I realized I lived in a bubble. All my friends were married, and I just thought there were no decent guys out there. I did meet some men who actually astonished me with their sincerity and sweetness. It takes time, though, to shop around. I am sure many of you, like me, after trying on 30 bathing suits have given up and thought how fat they all make us look. Then you return in a week or two, and suddenly find three or four you like. Now, you have to narrow it down further and choose one. What a difference attitude and timing can make. This is true whether it is investing or relationships.

This whole book is designed to help you change your attitude toward money. I want you to view money, when used wisely, as your friend and not your jailer. Timing is the key that opens the door or unlocks your potential.

How much time do each of us spend agonizing over when he is going to call or checking emails to see if he has sent a note? Let's make a commitment now to change. Tomorrow keep track of how much time you spend worrying about "him" and see how disruptive it is to our whole day. I hate it! Suddenly, I turn into this little high school girl who doesn't want to leave her phone or computer, in hopes he may call. I can be in complete control over every aspect of my life until boys enter the picture. Suddenly, I revert to a 13 year old. Do you really think he spends the same amount of time agonizing over us? NEVER! He is probably at his computer right now checking his portfolio balance and worrying about the money he lost in the market today instead of when to call us. Let's start doing the same.

6

The Past Doesn't Lie!

"We live in the present, we dream of the future,

but we learn eternal truths from the past."

- Madame Chiang Kai-Shek

There are reasons why certain statements stay around forever. They will forever be true. 'The past doesn't lie' is one of these statements. It may seem overused and trite, but it is honest. Don't ignore the past. Past behavior is a key indicator for future action. This is true with men and money!

My friend called me up this week and said, "Don't date a man's potential." What does this mean? At least in my mind, I start fantasizing about how this person is going to be, as soon as we feel chemistry. I see all his potential. I start asking myself, "Is the search finally over? Could this really be Mr. Right?" I quickly begin dreaming of our big future together, because I somehow feel a sign that fate has brought us together. I erase from my mind the present, where he hasn't called recently or doesn't communicate easily. Our lives still seem compatible, but there are things that make me wonder. I have made my list of qualities that I can't live without, and the number one quality my companion must have is laughter. The strange thing is, I haven't heard him laugh once, and he hasn't made me laugh, yet. How can I ignore that fact? Laughter is the magic that gets you through the tough times in a relationship.

Now, some women change the story a bit. Just because he cheated on his last girlfriend or wife, doesn't mean he will cheat on me. Hmmm, let's wait a few months and see the ending . . .

So, what else do we know from the past? People get sick, injured or die. I am not going to glamorize this fact. Right now we are going to discuss insurance because this is one of the most important ingredients you need to protect you, your family and your future. Here are five valuable insurance products:

Five types of Insurance

Life insurance—Whole Life and Term

Long-Term Care insurance

Disability insurance

Homeowners Insurance

Personal Umbrella Policy

Some of my background in the financial industry is in the insurance part of the industry. As a result, I have a pretty good knowledge of life insurance. I have sat through endless hours of training classes. It is disturbing to me that many well-known people who offer financial advice, make blanket statements telling everyone to buy term insurance and invest the rest. This is **not** always the right answer, and I will show clear examples.

Why do you buy life insurance?

You buy life insurance if you love someone. This sounds silly, but it is true. We have had people come into our office and say they don't feel like they need to leave anything to anyone and their kids need to fend for themselves in life. They have raised them and they have their own jobs. Now the kids are "on their own". These individuals want to enjoy **all** their money and not worry about saving any for anyone else. These people are probably not going to buy life insurance.

Life insurance is a gift you buy to protect the ones you love. If someone dies unexpectedly, life insurance helps them maintain their current lifestyle (hopefully.) I put in the word hopefully because it depends on the amount you purchased. Please be smart about who you purchase life insurance from. If a life insurance agent comes to talk to you and recommends you purchase $300,000 of term insurance without telling you how he came up with that figure, please run. People often come into our office with two or three different life insurance policies and have no idea why they purchased the specific amount they did. We never recommend a specific amount until after we have gone through the whole fact finding process. It is important to know how much it takes for them to live currently, and then factor in other aspects, like childcare and whether they want the house paid off for the surviving spouse. Only then will we recommend a specific value.

Another big mistake couples make is only buying insurance on the man, if the wife is a stay at home mom. He believes that if his wife passes on, nothing will change that much. He doesn't put a financial value on her. On NBC Nightly News this year, an interesting statistic was released. If you had to buy the services of a stay at home mom in 2008, her services would have come to a value of $99,000 in monetary terms. (Now women, I know this number may disappoint some of you because you know your services are priceless, but this is a good first step in the right direction.) The news report said that if a working mother passed on, her additional services would be worth $76,000. You may wonder what the difference is for. The working parents may pay for a cleaning service or childcare, while the stay at home mom provides that until she becomes disabled or dies. It in no way means that one is better than another!

Women need to learn to stand up for themselves and realize how emotionally and financially valuable they are to a family! I hope I never see another man walk into my office and say that the wife doesn't need life insurance. That is an absolute lie that needs to change NOW.

Whole Life versus Term Insurance

Okay, what is the difference between term versus whole life insurance? The most common way to explain it is renting versus owning. Term insurance is like renting an apartment. It costs a lot less that owning a house, but after your lease is up, you don't have anything to show for it. Whole life is like owning a home, because it costs more but also increases in value over time. You receive a lot of tax advantages that you don't with term. Your money will revert back to your estate and grows tax-deferred.

In these difficult economic times, whole life insurance can be a wonderful product. It is one of the few products that will offer you a death benefit that never drops in value (the stock market sure can't say that) and keeps growing in cash value. It can also protect money from creditors. Yes, whole life insurance policies are completely protected from creditors. It is probably horrible to repeat this, but many builders, through the advice of their lawyers, have recently put enormous amounts of money in whole life policies. They love this product because their money is safe, grows over time and remains safe from creditors. It is okay to learn from the wealthy tricks that help preserve assets.

What I like about whole life insurance is that you "become your own bank." Within a few years of owning your policy, you can take money out of your life insurance policy without a penalty, because the "cash value" of a policy has grown. People have taken money out as a down payment on a house, to pay a tax bill or go on vacation. When you are your own bank, you are self-sufficient. You don't have to argue with a loan officer at a bank, you have the power and make the decisions. We will talk about disability insurance soon, but you quickly get the feeling of "being your own bank."

Ok, I won't lie that whole life insurance costs a lot more than term, so it is out of reach to many people. I think the idea of buying term and investing the rest is good, but the reality of it rarely happens. Usually some emergency comes up and the extra money is never invested. I just want you to keep whole life in the back of your mind, so if you get a large inheritance or some wonderful promotion, please consider it. You can set up policies so many different ways, including a lump sum payment. This set-up would be desirable if you just received a large sum of money and wanted to make sure it never lost its value.

Be very careful though. If you are going to invest in a life insurance policy, please buy from a company that is high quality. You want it to still be in existence when you need the money. I currently am an insurance broker for one of the three remaining "mutual" companies. This company has been in existence over 150 years and has a AAA rating. (That is the best of the best.) This rating is higher than any bank or brokerage/investment firm has. Why? These mutual companies are not publicly traded. This means that the mutual companies are less risky because they are governed by the policyholders. They don't have to make risky investments, worry about their returns, or be concerned about "shareholders" anger if the value of their stock drops.

Buying insurance should be a similar mind set to how we think when we go shopping. There are a few articles of clothes I am willing to spend a little more on, because they are very important in my life—like my running shoes. I had one client who would not spend more than $4.00 on any article of clothing for her or her children except for her running shoes. She loved to run and didn't want her knees to be ruined so she splurged and got really nice running shoes. This woman is one of my favorite examples of the ultimate bargain shopper. She always looks amazing when you see her. You would never know all her clothes were bought at consignment stores. She is a single parent with four children and one has special needs. Nothing has deterred her and she *knows* the value of a dollar! We need to stop throwing away money on things without lasting value, and invest smartly for a better future.

Remember how we talked earlier about each investment product meeting two out of three financial goals. Insurance offers safety and growth, but it offers very little liquidity.

Long-Term Care Insurance

One of the biggest challenges in selling insurance is dealing with health issues. I have so many clients who want to buy life insurance or long-term care insurance, but they cannot get it because they have too many health issues.

Many people tell you to wait until your 50's and 60's to buy long-term care insurance, but that has recently created a lot of challenges. At these ages people are on so many medications or already have so many health issues, no one will "underwrite" them or issue them a policy. Please don't wait to buy long-term insurance! I hate to tell you, but I even have women clients in their early forties who have been turned down for long-term care.

What is long-term care insurance and why buy it? Long-term care insurance has often been known as a product only the really wealthy purchase, but that is now changing. Long-term care insurance is an amazing product because it offers people choices as they get older. They are eligible for long-term care if they cannot do two out of the five normal daily activities, which are: bathing, dressing, eating, transferring (able to get out of bed) or relieving themselves. When this situation occurs, many people need to move into a facility or get in-home assistance. Most people would like to stay in their home, as long as possible. Unfortunately, this is very expensive. In North Carolina, in-home care can cost $30.00 an hour which could total anywhere from $500 to $700 a day. That could eat through your savings quickly, especially if your goal is to save some money for your children! Cost for full time care in facilities can range from $150 to $300 a day. You can do the math but that could quickly become $9000. per month ($300x30) or $108,000. a year. This doesn't include the cost of inflation, so these numbers could rise quite a bit in a few years. (Please also note that this expense could be much higher in your state. Prices vary greatly depending on location.)

Widows often are the number one purchasers of long-term care insurance, because they don't want to be a "burden" on their children. Widows don't want the kids to worry about how to care for them if they lose their mobility. Insurance can help bring everyone peace of mind.

Purchasing long-term care insurance can seem confusing. Agents will ask you how you want your policy designed. In the past, you would usually buy a daily benefit, but now the companies are selling a monthly benefit. I would recommend the monthly benefit because some days you may not need care or have family visiting, while on others you may need additional care through the night. This policy allows for flexibility. Agents will also ask you if you want simple or compounded inflation. Simple inflation means that the monthly benefit amount will rise each year on a simple or flat rate—like 3%. A compound inflation rate changes each year based on current inflation; so your monthly benefit will keep up with the rising costs of healthcare. Compound inflation costs more. Which choice is right for you? This decision depends a lot on the client's age. If you are under the age of 60, we recommend compound insurance. It usually requires you owning the policy for nine to ten years for compound inflation to be the better choice. After ten years, compound inflation almost always wins as the most cost effective choice.

Disability Insurance

When we talk to clients, everyone knows they have disability insurance through work but *NO* one has ever known how much it is for, unless we make them go back to human resources and ask. They assume they are automatically protected.

Did you know that more people become disabled than die before the age of 65?

This fact was listed in the National Safety Council in 2003. 1 in 5 people will be disabled for one year or more before age 65, states Compton Insurance Marketing in 2002, along with the fact disability is the cause of nearly half of all home foreclosures in the US states. Again, no one thinks it will happen to them! They figure they are protected if they become disabled. The reality is the exact opposite. Your whole world can come crashing down right in front of you. Do you really think any bank is going to issue a loan to someone who just became disabled? NO! Doors you never expected will start slamming in your face. This is again one of the reasons we discussed whole Life Insurance.

Please remember that almost all disability claims are turned down the first time by Social Security. As a result, it will be a very lengthy process to get money immediately. With no personal savings, like the average American, your financial future could start crumbling away quickly. Even A Group Disability Insurance through work won't solve everything. It typically only pays 45-60% of annual income upon the claim, reports JP Morgan in January of 2004.

Disability insurance through work is not enough. It can be frustrating trying to sell disability insurance, because there are many people who do not meet the requirements of insurance companies. Most small business owners cannot purchase disability insurance until they have been in business for two years. Also, they must be earning an income. This leaves many people without coverage. There are still ways to protect yourself through buying certain forms of term insurance, but you need to plan ahead!

Homeowner's Insurance

Home. The center of life. I often think it is indestructible, especially when I see how my boys body slam in the house, but it is not. Everything in my house is connected with a memory. Before I get into the importance of the correct homeowner's insurance, I want you to promise me you will take anything that you can't live without and put it in a safe. (Hopefully, it will fit.) For example, in a bank safe I have my wedding ring and my husband's ring, for my kids to use some day. I also have a videotape of my husband's service so my kids will always have a copy. After Hurricane Katrina, emergency officials said to make sure your passport and social security card were in a safe, because they are the only way to verify who people were. I also have $1,000.00 hidden in my house. This is because people rush banks when the news breaks of a possible hurricane or tornado. If I have to leave town immediately, I want to have money so I can afford the basics of life, such as food and water. Remember, it was a long time before most banks were reopened in New Orleans.

I think that buying homeowner's insurance is a "no brainer" that I don't need to dwell on. Most homeowners must have it, if they carry a mortgage, so I am going to focus on the two big mistakes that people make.

First, they don't know when their insurance does NOT cover damages to their home. I had a rude awakening when I started asking what my homeowner's insurance would not cover. For example, my home is not covered for flood insurance. I live in a special flood plain so the only way I can carry flood insurance is to get an additional rider that is expensive. Each of us has to weigh our choices. That rider wouldn't seem very expensive compared to the price of rebuilding my house, so each of us has to decide when the extra money is well-spent. It is amazing how often our homes are not covered for hurricanes or fires. Please call your agent and find out all the facts so you are informed.

Wouldn't it be nice if we could call an ex of one of the guys we are dating and find out the whole story about how she was treated? It is always hard to make a decision if we only know one side of the story.

The second big mistake is not to know the replacement value that has been placed on your home. If your home is destroyed tomorrow, what value would it cost to rebuild it? Sometimes, insurance companies only insure your home for the value of it when you bought it. They don't take into account the difference in cost if your home burns down three years later. The cost of home-building materials is always on the rise. Make sure your policy adjusts the replacement value to include not only the original cost, but the new cost with inflation.

Personal Umbrella Insurance

I am absolutely shocked at how rarely this insurance is discussed, how cheap it is and how valuable it can be. No one had ever told me about this insurance until I was in my 30's. My husband was a state representative and a very public figure. I decided I wanted to look into personal coverage to protect my family because sometimes you run into a crazy constituent. You never know what people will try to sue people for next. My insurance agent, who handles all my homeowner's insurance and auto insurance, said I could get one million or 2 million dollars of umbrella insurance for around $30 a year. I couldn't believe it! Why is this coverage important? If you got in a car accident, your auto insurance would cover damage claims against you to a certain point-maybe one million dollars. If you permanently injured other people, they could try to get additional money and could try to go after your personal assets. Umbrella insurance protects your assets in these instances. Over time, this additional protection, at such a low rate, could really save your family from major loss.

To be a bargain shopper in the insurance industry, it is important to bundle your home, auto and personal umbrella with one company. Also, don't forget to shop around at least every two years. I saved well over $1,000.00 by switching companies less than two years ago.

Remember, don't forget the lessons of the past. Many of my mistakes with money and men I have had to learn with a high price tag attached to them. I share my stories only in hopes of saving you some suffering along the way. Now it is time to talk the talk, so you can walk the walk. Read on . . .

7

Having the Tough Conversation

"There is no rule that life has to be hard.

I looked it up."

- Lora Canary, Owner

Creative Customer Connections

"We need to talk." Some of the most feared four words in the English language. Need I say more? We have all sat on both sides of it and have dreaded every word. Is the "talk" ever enjoyable? Rarely, but is it absolutely fundamental in every relationship? **YES!** At least if you want to keep moving forward and care about the future. We all know there is no perfect moment for the talk. No bell will sound or door shut to tell us the time is NOW. What does make the talk easier is planning.

This is a topic that is close to my heart since I am a widow and financial planner. Right before my husband passed on at 35 years old, I had to have the dreaded "talk" with him in which I had to ask him questions like "Do you want a service? Would you like to be cremated?" The talk was dreadful only because our last moments were spent asking difficult questions about his death rather than enjoying our last few moments together. I wish I could stop time right now and go back. All of us think we are invincible and this will never happen to us. It can! This is why I am so passionate as a financial planner. I don't want anyone else's final conversation to be the same one I had with my husband.

Having the talk should never destroy a relationship but instead build new levels of intimacy and commitment. More couples divorce over **money** than over any other issue. Why? The answer is that most women hate to discuss touchy subjects or heated topics. Together, we are going to discuss how to approach these tough conversations tactfully and lovingly whether it is your boyfriend, husband or parent. Certain general rules apply.

Step one: The Right Environment is essential.

About three months before my husband passed on, my mother wanted to confront my husband and beg him to slow down his campaign and take care of himself. (He had known he had cancer and was re-elected one month before he died.) She thought I had not spoken firmly enough to my husband about the importance of his role in our family as a father and husband. She came over on a Sunday afternoon and we called him home from campaigning to talk to him bluntly. This approach was horrible! He was first mad because we called him away from the campaign trail and he hated being surprised. He very quickly got bitter and resentful about this topic even being discussed. My mother and I were scared that he would not talk to us if we had tried to schedule a time to talk with him. Looking back, I know it would have been the more loving thing to do.

Step Two: Listen.

This talk is not about **you** but learning where the other person stands, what their goals are, and how they plan to achieve them. You may not want to hear all the answers right now, but it is better now than further down the road. If you don't see eye-to-eye, then it is time to see if you can find a middle ground.

I have been amazed by how many people have gone into a marriage without an understanding on religion or children. These are major issues that need to be discussed and decided before entering into marriage. I know too many people who have had marriages break up because one person wanted kids while the other did not. Marriage is not going to suddenly solve all your problems. You need to hear what your partner is saying about his or her feelings before entering marriage. Most people do not change their ways after getting married but they probably do the opposite and get more firmly embedded in their beliefs.

Step Three: Be courageous!

Open communication takes courage, and it is essential not only to a strong relationship with yourself and your finances, but also to your family. I have to live forever with my husband's family (whom I adore), but we had some rocky times to go through. Sitting in a hospital room with different family members, all having their own opinions on what to do next with my husband's care, I now understand why you need documents like durable health care and durable power of attorney. It is so easy to see how the Terry Schivo case could happen again. The repercussions of not having the "talk" can be far reaching and last a lifetime. We all know families where relatives or even siblings have never spoken again after the passing of a parent or loved one.

If you are going to talk to your parents or loved ones, especially about their final wishes, please tell them beforehand, so they can be thinking about it. My sister emailed her in-laws a list of around 10 to 15 questions to consider concerning their desires. It was not practical to go visit them, because they lived many states away. Then they found a time for a telephone call to go over the answers together. If you are going to talk about estate planning, please find a comfortable place where both parties feel at ease with the conversation.

Important Legal Questions to Ask

Do you have a current Will?

Who has a copy of it?

What lawyer executed the Will for you?

If you become less mobile at some time in the future, what are your wishes?

Do you want to stay in your house as long as possible?

When you can no longer care for yourself, do you want to go to a care facility?

Is there a specific care facility you want to go to?

If you have pets, you may want to ask what they want to be done with their pets, if the care facility will not allow them.

Do you have long-term care insurance or any money set aside to offset the cost of long-term care?

If money runs out to pay for your stay at a specific care facility, would you like us to sell the house?

Have you written down your final wishes, such as whether you want to have a private service just for family at home, or a larger service at a church? Are there any specific hymns or music you would like played? Do you know who you would like to speak at or conduct the service?

Have you made any final arrangements such as buying a burial plot or do you want to be cremated? If you want to be cremated, where do you want your ashes scattered?

If they have not written down their final wishes, please ask them. Then either send a copy to your siblings or leave it with their Will.

Have you made a list of any personal items that you want to go to specific people, such as a piece of jewelry or a picture? The attorney should have this.

Here is the list of important legal documents you need to have:

Will   This is a legal document that only goes into effect *after the death of* the individual that states how the individual wants their property to be distributed. A Will is less costly and works best in situations where there will not be large battles over the distribution of property or concern over large estate taxes, because the deceased's assets would have to go through probate court.

Revocable or Irrevocable Living Trust

A living trust has become a popular substitute for a Will. A trust is set up while an individual is alive and assets can be transferred to it to save on taxes. All the money in a trust never goes to a probate court so it remains private. People with larger estates usually choose this option. Revocable trusts means that you can alter trustees and other elements of the trust while you are alive. Irrevocable means that the trust cannot be changed in any way.

A Living Will

Different from a Will, this document is used only when individuals are alive and in a terminal or vegetative state. It offers medical direction on how they want to be treated when they cannot properly communicate their desires.

Durable Power of Attorney	This document states who has the right to act on your behalf in legal and business matters, if you are unable to.
Durable Powers of Attorney for Health Care	This document is usually used along with the living will. It specifically grants one person the right to make the final decision on your health care needs.

Choices you need to make before talking to a lawyer:

Guardian	The person or couple who will care for your children in the event you or you and your spouse die.
Executor	The person you designate to carry out your wishes as stated in your Will.
Trustee	The person appointed by you to manage and distribute the assets of your Trust as it dictates.

Please make the guardian and trustee two different people. Unfortunately, I have been told too many scary stories of situations in which the guardian of a child used the money designated to raise the child for his/her own debt or personal needs. I hate to even say this, but these have been documented over and over!

Beneficiaries   People or organizations that receive the specific property or assets designated by you in a Will, Trust or in a financial contract such as an insurance policy or Roth IRA.

Pre-Nup   Legal contract created before a marriage that provides for the division of property and assets in the event of a death or break up of marriage. This can also include agreements for spousal support when a marriage is terminated.

Let me flip the tables for a minute. I have a guy friend who is the eternal optimist about love. He falls hard and fast for girls, often making them run because of his show of intense, premature emotion. I have frequently heard his tales of woe, because he thought he had found "the one." With one woman, the two decided to buy a house and move in together. Here the problems began, and so did the never-ending legal battle. The house was bought by both of them, but each of them did not put in the same amount of money. When they broke up, this fact was quickly forgotten. For over three years, the legal battles have waged. She won't speak to him. He can only communicate with her brother, because the arguments have escalated into many nasty threats.

Please have the foresight to create a back-up plan and legal contract if a house is bought when you are living with a person and not married to them. It may save you endless heartache and allow you to move forward in life much faster than my friend, who could be forced to declare bankruptcy soon.

8

Trust Your Gut

"The trouble is that not enough people have
come together with the firm determination
to live the things which they believe in."

- Eleanor Roosevelt

I turned on The Oprah Show this week while writing this book in isolation. She had a deeply disturbing interview where a woman was about to go before a jury because she killed her husband who was a policeman. When she called domestic help hotlines, she was told her only option was to first *save money* and then *permanently disappear*. Her whole reason to come on the show was to warn women that at the first signs of controlling behavior—RUN! Don't allow anyone else to have complete control of you or your money. Women always need to keep money of their own.

Remember the first advice the domestic hotline gave her. Save money! I will repeat again what I said in the first chapter—that money is power. Don't give away your power to another person! Yes, your man may seem perfect at the beginning of the relationship, but things can unfortunately take a turn for the worse. This woman said that it was four years into their relationship when he started displaying this abusive behavior. From there it escalated over time.

Saving money saves lives! Women, it is time to stop spending and save. Let's analyze why we shop, and how to stop impulsive spending. Together we can develop a budget that will work with our lifestyle so you can stay in control. You may think this discipline is not important for you right now, but someday it may save your life!

When I came into my current job, an older man in my office sat me down to tell me a few realities of men and money. He said, "Leslie, there is not a man I know who does not have a secret stash of money hidden away that his wife knows nothing about. If you ask, he will deny it to his grave, but it is true. He said women need to get smarter and have their own hidden money that their husband knows nothing about." How about that wake-up call, women?

Women are "givers." We want approval from others to help our self-esteem that can falter at times. We think that by giving to others, it will always come back to us. One of my closest friends is the "ultimate" giver. She will treat for dinners, throw lavish parties and has even given my kids new clothes. The funny thing is that she never understands that I would be her friend no matter what. It has never been about her "giving" me things. What has troubled me the most recently is learning her true financial picture. She has no business really "giving" to anyone. She needs to just stop spending and protect her current assets for her and her family, or it will ruin her financially. I have even been told she has a boyfriend who she treats for everything. She is so scared of losing love that she may end up losing herself in the process.

In her gut, she knows this lifestyle has to end. She even acknowledges the boyfriend is not the "one" but she is too scared to be alone. Here is the point where courage has to step in. I don't know how to avoid the subject of God in this book so if I offend, I am sorry. We all have to see that financial and emotional peace walk hand in hand. If one is out of balance in your life, the other usually is too. On the front of our Sunday school it states, "God is Love." What does that mean? God loves you and only wants good for you. God is everywhere or "All-in-All." Even if you step out of a bad relationship, you can't lose Love. Love may show itself in different forms to you like new friends and close family, but you can't lose a thing. You can't ever lose God so you can't lose Love.

I can promise you these facts are true. After losing my dad at 15 and then my husband at 35, I have had to turn to a higher sense of Love. On the front of our church are two sayings I reflect on often. One is from Jesus, "And ye shall know the truth, and the truth shall make you free." (John 8:32) Facing and confronting the Truth, whether it is overspending, staying in a bad relationship, or hating your job, will bring you freedom—freedom emotionally and financially. Think how much money people would save if they stopped drinking, smoking, or gambling. Aren't these three acts tied to finding temporary solace in material pleasures? Most of the time your current course just leads you to more sadness or turmoil.

The second saying on our church wall states, "Divine Love always has met and always will meet every human need." (Science and Health with Key to the Scriptures by Mary Baker Eddy) How does this relate to you? Another person, job, or pair of cute shoes will **never** meet all of our human needs, but God will. There are only two requirements: listen and follow. Your gut or spiritual intuition is telling you what is the next right step. You just need the courage to listen and follow it. I know this doesn't often happen overnight. You may not instantly master a budget for yourself. I know I didn't, but slowly you learn what works and what doesn't. I stayed in one relationship almost a year longer than I should have for so many wrong reasons. Step by step you must bring your life under control, just like your budget.

Now, I really want to focus on what often keeps us from developing a proper budget:

Fear.

Time.

Entitlement.

Maturity.

Accountability.

Let's look at these in more detail:

Fear

Avoidance can seem a lot easier than dealing with reality. Doing laundry and washing dishes may even look good versus creating a budget. Why? Because we have to face the facts. We know we overspent and lived beyond our means, but it doesn't seem as real when we don't put a dollar figure on it. The United States Government has a $12,000,000,000,000 (trillion) deficit. Yours can't be that bad. Remember it is okay to start with baby steps. My first step was buying a cute black and white plaid journal to track my expenses. I knew I would keep it with me if I liked what it looked like. Then I vowed to track my daily expenses each day. This includes even your daily cup of coffee or tea from Starbucks, or the tip you gave to the man at the airport. Everything!

Time

Where does it always seem to go? I have the best of intentions to get my to do list done each day, but it never gets completed. In The Woman's Advantage Shared Wisdom Calendar, I received this helpful advice by Brenda Novak, "Each day, do the thing you dread most first, then every other goal will be easy." This advice really works well. I have used it often. Remember that there is a large initial amount of time required to develop a budget, but maintaining it is not as hard. It is just like setting up automatic bill pay on your accounts. It seems like such a hassle to get it all in place, but over time it saves you countless hours of writing checks and lots of money because you don't use postage mailing all those bills. I hope you have all done that! The other great budgeting trick that I believe is helpful is getting "even-pay" put on your bills that can fluctuate seasonally, bills for energy, water and gas. This allows me to know for sure how much I owe each month, instead of just making a wild guess based on an estimate from the last twelve months.

Where should you start? Spend the next month collecting all your statements that are mailed to you. Place them in a folder, so you don't forget anything. Each day print out one or two pieces of information that you will need from your computer. At the end of the year, your credit card company should give you an annual summary. They even categorize your expenses. You will need that summary. Often the card company will categorize expenses incorrectly so you might appear to be over-weighted in miscellaneous, but this is a real wake up call. I was shocked to see last year what I spent on travel. (Oops, you found out my secret. I have a really bad travel bug!)

You need to go online and find a budget that you like as an example, or ask your financial adviser for one. Personally, I have used Dave Ramsey's because it is so in depth. I would have forgotten my kid's haircuts or gifts for school teachers, if it weren't for him. Suze Orman offers a budget as do many websites such as MassMutual. I'm not going to develop another budget form because other people have worked hard on them. I want to focus more of my time looking at the emotional reasons that stop you from doing or maintaining a budget. I know you can live by a budget if you finally put your mind to it.

Entitlement

I just landed a big account or my kids just got their grades from school, so it's time to celebrate. Right? Isn't that worth a nice dinner or a free Nintendo DS game for my kids? Who cares if it isn't in the budget? We will figure it out later. Sometimes you just have to let loose. Isn't it this sense of entitlement that has gotten our country in trouble? We have gotten to a point as parents where it is easier to say "yes", than to have to argue at length because we said "no." This is a mistake that needs to stop with this generation!

The economic downturn may have been a good thing in relation to people finally learning to stop this sense of entitlement. With so many spouses out of work, people have had to learn to bargain shop and stop buying the "extras." Eating meals out should not be the norm, but a rare treat or exception.

Do we still go into stores and see things we want? Yes, of course. Slowly we are learning to say "no" and walk away.

You just can't get everything because you want it or because someone said that dress would look perfect on you.

One of the best ways to stop shopping is to become a single parent. I don't have time, even if I wanted to, to walk in a store and shop! My dream night out is the thought of going to the grocery store without kids. I can't tell you the last time I went in a mall and just walked around.

Maturity

The most important lesson I learned from Dave Ramsey is that mature adults learn a sense of delayed gratification. Mature adults don't buy things they can't afford. They take the time to save the money, negotiate a bargain, and then pay with cash. He also has a rule that you should not buy a large ticket item (You can determine the value—some people chose $100, others $300) when you see it. Instead, you should go home and wait twenty-four hours before you go back and purchase it.

I hate to tell you how many times I hid purchases from my husband when we were married because I didn't want him to get mad because I had gone shopping. I would wait until he was at work to bring in my purchases, or hide them in my office. If you have to hide your purchases from your spouse, that probably is not healthy or mature behavior. The funny thing is I realized that many women do that. I was not alone. I will always be a proponent of separate bank accounts and keeping one joint account for household expenses. Each spouse has a right to some "blow it" money. This is money that each individual has a right to spend on whatever they want without judgment from the other spouse, as long as it is not more than was budgeted. That represents maturity and a healthy freedom. If you want something that is more expensive than the money allotted, then you need to save for a few months to buy it. These can be wonderful teaching times for your children. No one gets what they want all the time.

Accountability

This can be one of the scariest and most important lessons you learn in life. I think all of us hate being accountable to someone for all of our actions. In the financial industry we also have to deal with compliance issues. Madoff has made such a bad reputation for our industry. It is amazing to me how his actions went for decades without being discovered. Our industry requires more and more paperwork each day because we must be accountable for all the decisions we make with our clients' money.

Managers have a very important job making people accountable and often teaching employees that to earn people's respect, you must show up early for a meeting, not just on time. I will always remember my first date with a guy who I dated for a few months. He showed up around five minutes late begging for forgiveness. He was sweating because he had run all the way across a shopping center after he discovered he was in the wrong spot. I just couldn't stop laughing, because most people don't care that much if they are late. While we dated, he never showed up late again. He was always early or exactly on time. I realized what an amazing maturity this habit showed. It was easier for him because he didn't have to worry about kids! One day, I even called him to warn him of an accident that was slowing up traffic because I didn't want him to be late. He told me he always leaves early enough to allow time for accidents. He had learned from one of his first sales managers who would fire people if they showed up late. The manager didn't listen to the excuse even if it was something with your child or a car breaking down. Honestly, it showed me how important being on time is in showing people you are dependable and trustworthy. This man was the top of the top in selling. I doubt if I will never know someone more efficient and reliable.

Have I never ever been late? No, but I am learning a lot more about allowing proper time for the unknowns in life. I want to be a person people see as always reliable and accountable. Being a single parent has helped me gain a new sense of maturity and accountability, because there is no one else to fall back on. You set the example for your kids. What type of characteristics do you want to teach them? Discipline and accountability are important traits they will need for life.

Each small step you take in becoming more accountable is a step closer to success and your goal of financial stability. By stopping your excess spending, you have money to save. Save for your future and your children's future if there is money available. How much should you be saving? The general rule is you should be saving at least 10 to 15% of your income. This may need to be higher if you are getting closer to retirement.

127

The statistics are amazing about how much easier it is to save if you start young.

Patrick Kelly gives a perfect example in "Tax-Free Retirement":

There are two individuals named Jill and Mark. Jill sets aside $2000.00 a year and stops investing after eight years when she is 26. She lets her $16,000 grow at 10% compound interest rate until age 65. Mark waits until he is 27 to contribute $2000 a year, but he continues each year until he retires at 65. His contribution over 39 years is $78,000. Who do you think has more? Mark started contributing eight years after Jill, but he contributed a whole lot more. The difference is remarkable. Jill's initial investment had grown to $1,035,160 while Mark's is worth only $883,185.

Think of how you can change the lives of your children if you start setting aside just a little bit of money for them while they are young. Then encourage them to save, especially while they are single.

Can't you just walk with your back a little straighter now that you know you are moving in the right direction? You can feel yourself exuding more confidence on the outside. Oh, I better not give away any secrets from the next chapter. You'll have to keep reading . . .

9

Confidence is Key

"Women who are confident of their abilities
are more likely to succeed than those who lack
confidence, even though the latter may be much
more competent and talented and industrious."

- Dr. Joyce Brothers

Do you own a red dress? Have you learned how to enter a room feeling completely confident? We all know women who know how to command an entrance, no matter where they are. They have an aura about them, a confidence that is unmistakable. This confidence is not learned overnight. It takes time to develop. I have finally learned to feel confident no matter what environment

I am in, with or without a date. Through Toastmasters, I am also working on perfecting my public speaking. These last two years, I have confronted my fears, going to parties alone or speaking in public, instead of running from them. It has been wonderful to finally overcome many of these deeply embedded fears. You can, too!

One Saturday night when my friend ditched me, I finally realized how silly many of these false fears were. We were supposed to go see a movie and then I never heard from her. I was so mad that I wanted to leave her a nasty message, because I had gotten a babysitter and all. Well, I finally decided to go to the movie by myself. This seemed like the ultimate fear, going to a movie by yourself on a Saturday night. Why don't you just write loser across my forehead? Well guess what? I was fine. I honestly forgot all about being by myself and loved it. I even went out to eat in public after the movie. Some may be laughing, but this was a big step for me. I let go of so many silly fears that night. (Before I go further, I want to share with you that maturity also can be learning to bite your tongue, or waiting 24 hours before speaking your honest opinion. I was grateful I had done so this time. My friend had been in a car accident and no cell phones were allowed in the hospital.)

I want you to get rid of your silly fears, too, so you can **exude** confidence. You may be scared to death on the inside, which is fine, but on the outside I want you to realize how capable you are. Don't underestimate your ability. You have a very important role to play at work and home. We, as women, have a horrible inner voice that tries to demoralize us. I heard once that we think around ten thousand thoughts a day and over 90% are negative. Furthermore, 99% of the thoughts we think tomorrow are the same as the ones we thought today! It takes a lot of work to break this cycle of negativity. Start guarding your thoughts NOW, and work to allow good thoughts in. You will be surprised how much it changes your attitude, and soon your life.

How often have we been told to dress for your next job—the job you want? I want to tell you to dress yourself *mentally* and physically for the next job you want. You have to exhibit the qualities needed in a leader if you want to be a leader. Those qualities include confidence, responsibility, discipline, and organization. All of these can be seen and felt on the inside and outside.

Why is this important? Each step toward success gets you emotionally and financially closer to your goals. Each new career move leads to a higher salary and a higher sense of self-completeness. This recognition of self-worth manifests itself in more confidence. You are learning not to let other people push you around. You have an important voice that needs to be heard.

So now we are ready to discuss what to do with all the extra money you earn due to this new self-confidence. Do you put all your money in a 401(k) or are there other investment ideas to be considered, such as a Roth IRA?

People in the media preach over and over again to put as much money as you can into your 401(k) program. For understanding, I am going to say 401(k), even though I know that in the school system and non-profit work it is called a 403b, and also can be called a SEP IRA or TSA. The important thing to understand is why people say to invest in a 401(k). They tell you it defers or puts off paying taxes. This is true! The thing that is misleading is that they often tell you that it is saving you taxes. This is where you need to learn the **truth.** There is a short book that I am going to refer to often in the next two chapters called, "Learning to Avoid Unintended Consequences" by Leonard A. Renier. I would recommend it to everyone because it opens your eyes to many false myths you are frequently told For example, "It is always good to pay off your house as fast as you can."

A 401(k) program also defers the "tax calculation."* What does that mean? The 401(k)s was developed with the premise that when we retire we will be in a lower tax bracket than we are now. Nothing says that we will never owe the taxes. Please make sure you understand that fact. You will have to pay taxes on the money you invested at some point. The government does not care what tax bracket you were in when you originally contributed the money, only what tax bracket you are in when you take it out. No one can even tell you for sure how much you will save, because it is impossible to know what tax bracket you will be in, when you withdraw the money.

This 401(k) is designed with the idea that the government has formulated, that when you retire, you will be able to live off 60% of your current income. Let's just have a quick reality check. How many of us are living without debt on our current income today? If we are not presently debt-free, then do you think it is possible for you to live on only 60% of your income when you retire, especially since you probably want to travel and enjoy yourself? The myth involved in this design does not allow for changes in current tax brackets and increased inflation. Everything is going to cost more in the future.

Yes, let's buy into the idea that you could retire in a lower tax bracket, which means you win. The big problem is that you may not have the money at that time to pay the taxes. You would have done better paying the taxes in your high income earning days.

There is also an "opportunity cost" that we don't always evaluate. Opportunity cost is defined as "if you lose a dollar that you did not have to lose, you not only lost the dollar but also what that dollar could have earned for you if you had been able to keep it." So let's put this in simpler terms. If you spend $100.00 on the perfect dress, you not only lose $100.00 but you also lose the growth that you could have earned if you took that $100.00 and invested it. It could have easily become $5000.00 or even more in just a few years with the right investment.

The other important topic you must be aware of is the lack of liquidity. Remember, liquidity is based on how quickly and easily you can get your money out when you need it. We have many clients who have gotten into financial trouble. They are drowning in credit card debt! They want to take money out of their 401(k) so they can get back on their feet financially. Unfortunately, it is not that easy. Let's say you owe $30,000 in credit card debt. Can you just take out $30,000 from your 401 (k) and be done. NO! First, there is a 10% penalty for taking out money before the age of 59 1/2. Next, you will owe federal and state taxes on that money. Then, you have lost the opportunity cost of that money. We often see that people promise to change their ways after they take money out of their 401(k). They promise to repay it, but then another unexpected crisis occurs and they never do. That $30,000.00 they thought would be a quick fix has actually cost them thousands of dollars when it is time to retire. You can't easily make that up.

Now, am I telling you not to invest in a 401(k)? NO. What I want you to do is invest in a 401(k) to the maximum amount that the company will match, and then **stop**. The match of your company offsets your lost opportunity cost, but after that point, there are better investment choices. The numbers change each year, but for 2009 and 2010, you can invest up to $16,500 in your 401(k) if you are 49 and under, or $22,000 if you are 50 and above. Check and see at what point your company stops matching your contribution. This is important information— like learning that that perfect dress you loved is on sale for 50% at a store down the street. Why would you ever pay full price unless you didn't know? That is the same with 401(k).

So what are some better options for investing after you have put money in your 401 (k)? My first recommendation would be a Roth IRA. Why? A Roth IRA is a wonderful new investment tool that was created back in 1998. With this investment tool, the money you invest is taxed before you put it in. What does that mean? Unlike a 401(k), this money can be taken out when you retire without paying taxes on the amount. You can also take out the amount you invested in a Roth IRA at any time for an unexpected emergency without paying a tax penalty. The only money you cannot withdraw is the interest earned on the money invested. Unfortunately there are income limits and maximum contribution limits. In 2009, you can contribute $5000 if you are under fifty and $6000.00 if you are over fifty. Why doesn't everyone do this? Some people make too much money. You only qualify for a Roth IRA if you belong in one of the following categories:

Single: You earn less than $105,000 or between $105,000 and $120,000 adjusted gross income. What does this mean? If you earn $105,000 or less, you can contribute the full $5000 if you are under fifty, or the full $6000 if you are over fifty. If you earn between $105,000 and $120,000, you can contribute somewhere between $0 and $5000. You will need to consult an accountant for a more specific amount.

Married: You must file joint tax returns and earn less than$166,000 or between $166,000 and $176,000. Again this means if you both jointly make $166,000 or less, you can contribute the full amount of $5000 per person. If you both earn between $166,000 and $176,000, you can contribute between $0 and $5000 individually, but you will need to consult an accountant for a more specific amount.

When I was married, I contributed to my husband's IRA because he couldn't afford to. I was the beneficiary of his IRA when he passed on, so now I have the value of his IRA and mine combined. It can be helpful to contribute to your spouse's IRA for a specific time period if your spouse cannot afford to. Don't lose the tax advantage!

An exciting change has occurred in 2010. Please read this carefully. **In 2010, you can convert your IRA to a Roth IRA and take three years to pay the tax penalty for this change.** It is worth it! Why? Let's go over this again. In a Roth IRA, the money you invested is taxed when you invest it and grows tax-free. You will not be taxed on it even if it grows substantially over time, which we hope it does! With an IRA, the money you contribute is called "pre-tax dollars." You will be taxed on it when you take it out. Again, we assume the money will grow substantially, so you could face a hefty tax bill when it is taken out.

How should you contribute to your Roth IRA or IRA? Should you save up a large chunk of money until right before April 15 or should you contribute up to $500.00 per month? This can depend on your circumstances during the year. Some people save their Christmas bonuses and use them to pay their IRA contribution for the year. Many financial advisers urge you to contribute monthly because you will receive the benefit of dollar-cost averaging. What is that? It is the premise that over time, your money can grow faster if you invest slowly and steadily. The theory here is similar to the classic story of the tortoise and the hare. Slow and steady wins the race.

You will be surprised to see how a little money can grow over time. A few years ago, I stopped drinking anything but water when eating out because the average cost of soda was getting to be about $2. Please get up from your chair right now and do me a favor. Go online and look up "booze/beverage saving calculator". Enter the approximate cost of each drink you purchase and how many a day. It is absolutely amazing! Within a few years, you can easily save well over $100,000 by just drinking water. If you are a coffee drinker, look up "coffee saving calculator" on the internet. You can input the amounts that fit your lifestyle. Looking for an easy place to save money? You just found it! Not too painful.

I want you to have everything you dream of, but it comes with a price. You have to be smart with your money, mature

141

when making buying decisions, and disciplined when saving. It is a lot easier to "pay yourself first." This means having the money that you want to save each month automatically deducted from your account, before you see it or spend it. Then you are on the right track to keep moving ahead. Read on . . .

10

You Can Always Learn More . . .

"Woman must not accept; she must challenge."

- Margaret Sanger

If I want to learn how to communicate more effectively in a relationship, or how to write better, what do I do? I research the topic and try to learn more. If not, I just keep going around in circles. It is ground into our head at work that every financial planner must "invest" a few hours each day learning more. They must also study to keep up with the ever-changing laws and investment strategies that can help clients in this turbulent market. I can't assume recommendations I make for one client are beneficial and meet the needs of another client. Each case is unique and pushes me to learn new ideas. The financial industry is definitely one where people will fail if they don't keep informed about market changes and implement new strategies when appropriate.

This reminds me of the first date I went on after my husband passed on. I felt SO out of the dating loop and lost. This man was asking me questions that I never imagined like "Would you go back and change anything in your past?" or "What do you think is your best quality?" These questions were such a struggle for me because I had to look within myself and understand my feelings. I had to learn how I felt about the past and decide how to communicate my thoughts. I am sure I must have sounded so tongue-twisted. The funny thing is that I learned dating again could be an "okay" thing because I really had to learn who I was, what I wanted in life, and how to voice my concerns when I didn't think we were moving in the same direction. It was tough, but not as tough as the first kiss. This sounds funny, I know. I don't think you can ever forget your first kiss after you go through a divorce or get widowed. You've lived your whole life assuming you will never kiss anyone else but your spouse; then your world crashes. You really are unsure if you will ever love or kiss someone again. Then it happens. I was totally caught off guard! He kissed me. No it wasn't the perfect kiss, but you realize that is ok. You realize there is life after your husband dies. You really may love again, but it will take time. You are not there, but you have taken one small step and are starting anew.

In this chapter, we are going to discuss helpful ideas for when you need to buy a house or townhome or rent an apartment. After being widowed, one of the hardest things I had to learn quickly was how to buy and sell a house and negotiate contracts. (It probably didn't help that the real estate agent I hired kept hitting on me. Gross! I was just widowed, and that was the last thing on my mind.) First, I hate to say it but if you have a good guy friend, please grab him. I know a number of times my builder tried to rip me off because I was a single woman. I was so mad. I came into the final closing and the contract showed additional charges for carpeting and other expenses that he had said were included in the original price. I had to fight hard that day, and it made me sad that someone had tried to take advantage of me like that. I know a lot more now and won't make the same mistakes again. Why does it always take tough lessons to make us grow?

Sounds like some of our bad date stories. Huh? When I bought my last car, I decided to be smart. I had my guy friend, who works as a negotiator for a large company and has bought and sold cars in the past, buy my car. I also had two other friends who owned the car I wanted. I found out where they went to negotiate their deal, what they paid and the cost of extras that were thrown in. This time I came prepared. My guy friend carefully scripted me on what questions to ask and what questions not to answer, so I wouldn't lose negotiating power. For example, never tell a car salesman immediately if you are trading in your car or not. If they know that, then you lose negotiating power. They will be okay with selling you the new car for closer to invoice price, but then low-ball your trade in to make up the profit. They tried to pull some fast ones on me, but it didn't work. The information my friend had given me about how much he paid only a few months before gave me an edge. Remember, knowledge is power. I saw that.

You don't ever want to spend more than necessary in buying a new car. A new car instantly depreciates, goes down in value, by 20% as soon as you drive it off the car lot. People can lose more money buying cars over their lifetime, than in any other purchase, because a car depreciates every time you use it. A strong 8% return can look good in your 401(k) until you realize you are spending the same 8% on interest with your car loan. The loss or interest paid on the car loan counteracts the gain in the 401(k).

Author Leonard Renier writes, **"If something you thought to be true <u>wasn't</u> true, when would you want to know about it?** This question has been a big eye opener to me with home ownership and mortgages. My mother has always lectured me about paying off my house as soon as possible and trying not to have any debt. I have had to learn there is good debt and bad debt. Paying off your house **quickly** could be a poor financial decision. Let me please state that I would never tell you to not own your house outright later in life, but there are some important financial reasons to consider in not paying off your mortgage quickly. Why? Be patient with me because I will explain.

When we get a home mortgage, usually we make our decision based on the monthly payment amount and interest rate. If we can afford it, we often try to get a 15-year mortgage instead of a 30-year mortgage to save us all the interest.

We forget to factor in the other important issues like inflation, tax deductions, down payment, opportunity costs, liquidity, use and control. First, there is a wonderful video entitled, "Who holds this piece at your house?" In this video, we meet three couples. First, we meet the free-n-clears, who own their home outright and used cash to buy it. Next, we meet the pay-extras who couldn't afford to pay for the house outright, but are aggressively paying extra to get rid of the mortgage as soon as possible. Last, we meet the owe-it-alls who didn't even put a down payment on their house.

In this video, we learn key factors like the fact that your house appreciates the same whether you have paid it off or financed it 100%. So don't think that by paying cash your investment will appreciate more. It really is the exact opposite. Your house is one of the biggest investments you will make. In the companion book entitled, "Learning to Avoid Unintended Consequences", the author, Leonard Renier, shows the example of a couple who bought a house for $39,000 thirty-three years ago. Now they are selling it for $150,000. They are so excited because they believe they have a gain of $111,000. This would be a compound return of 4.17%. Unfortunately, the couple forgot to include the $53,000.00 they spent over the last 33 years for taxes and improvements. As a result, the gain was only $58,000.00 which results in only a 1.49% compound rate of return. That doesn't look so good any more does it?

Paying cash for a house may sound good because you feel powerful owning your largest investment, but we often forget about "opportunity cost." If you had taken that same $39,000.00 and invested it in the market, received the tax deductions for 33 years and still maintained some liquidity and control, I think you could have done better than a 1.49% return.

Paying off your home faster actually costs you money. Why? This is true because you are paying off your house with your most valuable dollars. Remember that it takes time to watch your money grow. The longer you have to invest, the more your money will grow. If you start investing later, it is almost impossible to catch up. People, who start investing after paying off a 15 year mortgage, never catch up financially to people who take the difference between a fifteen and 30 year mortgage and invest that amount for 30 years.

The book's author, Reneir shows that "if, rather than paying $150,000.00 cash for the house, you invested it instead at 7% for 30 years, it would grow to $1,217,475.00." That doesn't include around "$60,000.00 in tax savings in that 30 year period for someone in a 30% tax bracket."

The equity inside your home is growing at <u>zero</u> percent. The argument here is, "Well my house increased in value, therefore my equity went up." Well, whether you have $70,000.00 or $1.00 of equity, the value of the property would still have gone up. If property values went down, would you rather lose $1.00 or $70,000.00 of equity? Although we have been taught that our home is a safe place to park money, we really have to take a look at this situation. (Renier, page 83)

Let's use the example of a down payment to help clarify this:

Do you earn interest on your down payment?   No.

Do you have control of the money or does the bank?   Bank.

Does your down payment help with tax deductions?   No.

As a result, what do you think the ideal down payment should be? Zero. Your down payment is not yielding you any interest. Think about "opportunity cost." If you put that same amount of money in a money market fund, you would get better than zero! Of course, that is probably impossible with the current economic environment, but your goal is to make your down payment as low as possible, so you can invest your remaining money.

No one can take my house away if I own it. This is a powerful thought to people who have paid cash outright for their house. Unfortunately, this rug can quickly be yanked out from under your feet if someone becomes disabled or unemployed. All your cash is tied up in the house. If you suddenly become disabled and can't work, you lose your income. Social security will usually cover around 40% of your regular monthly expenses. You can't keep the bills paid with that. You go to a bank for a loan, but you can already guess their answer, especially in this tough economy where loans are already hard to come by. What do you do? It is difficult to depend on selling a house quickly. At this point you wish you were "your own bank." You wish you had easier access to your money. Disability is responsible for "48% of all foreclosures in the United States. Maintaining proper liquidity would prevent many financial calamities." (Reiner, page 87)

I have met with some widows who have received large insurance checks (not me, as you know, since we never had "the talk"). Their one desire is to have their home fully paid for, so it can't be taken away from them. They are scared! Their whole world has collapsed all around them and they don't know who to turn to and trust. Here is my first cautionary statement. Please don't do anything quickly. If you try to sell your house quickly, you will lose a lot of money. It is okay to take some time to heal. Just put the insurance money in a money market account for a few months. It is much better to do that than take a wrong step and lose money you will need to sustain your family in the future. Then, take the time to educate yourself. I may sound completely biased, but I would find a **woman** financial planner. They are going to be able to sympathize with and understand your emotions a lot more than men. Men think numbers, which is great, but a woman financial adviser will help you find the balance between peace of mind, security and protecting your future. I hate to say it, but still most men don't get it. They don't get our need for stability and security.

Home is where the heart is. That is what we are often told. Sometimes we cling too hard to our home. Women, this is especially true in the case of divorce. Women get jaded with thinking that as long as the kids and I stay in the house, that is ALL that matters. A lot of women have sacrificed hundreds of thousands of dollars because they had blinders on, as long as they got their home. I hate to tell you the reality, but most people move out of a house within five years after a divorce. Either the memories are too haunting or they can't afford to keep it up since they sacrificed almost everything else to keep the home. Your kids and you will survive even if you have to move. It may even make your kids more resilient in life. Challenges can bring a family closer.

My boys and I moved seven months after my husband passed on. I wanted to live closer to family. Was it easy? No! Would I do it again? Yes. Of course my kids were sad leaving behind their friends. My friends there were indispensable to me. I could never thank everyone in the community who stepped up to lend us a helping hand. It was absolutely incredible. I felt bad leaving everyone, but I wanted to look at the long-term picture. This was the best decision in the end—emotionally and financially.

Having all the memories in the house of my husband was just too overwhelming. I knew that the boys and I would drown in his memory instead of move forward. I want you to have the same courage to move forward in your life.

Don't let yourself or your family drown yourselves in a house you cannot afford. Let it go! It is really only a house. I will always remember a tape where a little girl easily got the true concept of home. The girl had moved endlessly before the age of ten. She said, "I always knew we had a home, we just sometimes didn't always have a house to put it in."

Remember it is time to do spring cleaning now. We are going through the closets and evaluating what we still need in life and what we can get rid of before we move forward. Sometimes, it may have to be the house we get rid of in order to move forward. I am here to reassure you that this decision is all right. Your kids can feel loved, regardless of where they are.

All of us need to watch the movie "Pursuit of Happyness" again. I remember coming home from watching the movie in the theatre, and then my mom exclaiming I must come see this interview on TV. The real individual whose life the movie was based on was on CNBC. The interviewer again asked him what his child remembered of the whole homeless experience. He said that his child remembered it as one of his happiest times, because they got to spend so much time together. Wow! Doesn't that put it all in perspective! It is not a fancy house or fancy toys that mean the most to kids. It is your **time**. If you are working two or three jobs just to stay afloat financially, please sell the big house. Your kids care more about being with you than any new toy or gadget. It goes back to time being money. You only have a limited amount of it, so spend it **wisely**!

Don't stop learning. You can learn new ideas everyday that will help you emotionally and financially. Maybe it is from reading a book, or chatting with a friend who made a stupid mistake that you can also learn from, or maybe it is just turning on CNBC. Stay present and live in the moment. Stop worrying about the future and learn what you need today to make the changes for a better tomorrow. We can't stop believing that we are all capable of changing and improving ourselves. So keep reading . . . we are almost finished with our journey together. I can't believe it!

11

Don't Stop Believing

"The greatest part of our happiness or
misery depends upon our dispositions,
and not our circumstances."

- Martha Washington

For one night this summer, time stood still. My old high school "crush" called and asked if I wanted to "hang out". It was the perfect night. He showed up in his cool convertible and we went "cruisin'" the back roads of a small town with The Steve Miller Band cranked up. He suddenly looked over at me and said, "Leslie, you know what the last chapter of your book should be, don't you?" I, of course, said, "No!" He replied, "You need to call it, "Don't Stop Believing." I liked it. Isn't it the truth? I can still replay in my mind many conversations with friends saying, "That's it. I am done with MEN! I am going to be a hermit forever. It is not worth the effort. I would rather be alone, than go through this endless roller coaster of love with its ups and downs."

So why do we always try again? Because we know we can't stop believing in ourselves and other people. I am the eternal optimist. In my heart, I believe that there is good in everyone, and that people can change. Isn't that why I am writing this book? I know for a fact how resilient women can be. We are strong and capable of doing anything we put our minds to. This book is just one small example of that. Each of us can make the changes we need emotionally and financially to become and find the "perfect" match. As we know, there is no magic formula or secret recipe for love or life. We have to learn as we journey on. Each tough experience becomes a stepping-stone, giving us courage to move forward. If we can handle growth, we can handle anything! I want this book to strengthen your belief in yourself, and give you the courage to achieve the balance we all need in life—the complete balance we need emotionally and financially.

Now, you have the tools you need for success. Unfortunately, they are useless unless you put them to work for yourself. Don't expect success instantly. It takes time, just like dating. I wish I never had to go on another first date again, but I also know it gets easier now. I have learned not to take things personally and move on when it is not right. Changing your financial lifestyle is going to be like that, too. You won't have a perfectly balanced budget instantly. We all hate credit card debt as much as we hate a blind date! Yet, we learn to face it and not be overwhelmed with it. Through time and persistent effort, it can be eliminated.

Recently, a friend encouraged me to read a book called, "the dip: a little book that teaches you when to quit (and when to stick)" by Seth Godin. I loved it, because it reminds us what the difference is between a "dip" and a "cul-de-sac". A dip is a "temporary setback that you will overcome if you keep pushing, while a "cul-de-sac" will "*never* get better, no matter how hard you try." Before we end this book, I want us to decide how we can "push" through our next temporary setback—like when we go out and buy the cute dress we really couldn't afford because we have a date with the cutest guy *ever*. Beating yourself up mentally is not the answer. Godin explains that "winners quit fast, quit often and quit without guilt" because "they realize that the bigger the barrier, the bigger the reward for getting past it." That's it!

Do you see it? It can seem absolutely overwhelming to get out of debt and start saving, but no one said it was easy. If it was easy, our country wouldn't be in such economic turmoil. Yet, think of the rewards of a life of emotional and financial peace. A life where you can guarantee that you and your children can live comfortably and reach all your goals, like owning your home and retiring without worries. Your money is not going to run out! You have your financial planner on speed dial! You have worked hard to maintain a close relationship with the planner, and changed your plan when it needed to be updated. This relationship, like any other, takes time and can't be neglected. We work hard for your money. Yet we don't take the same type of care and energy to protect and invest it wisely. Educating ourselves about money should be one of our absolute top priorities.

Let's review some of your homework assignments for the next 30 days:

Make a list of short term and long-term goals.

Here are mine:

Short Term Goals

1. Get this book edited and published so I can start my book tour!

2. Go back to using the envelope system for budgeting.

3. Work on being more consistent about rules with my children.

4. Try to keep my desk clean.

5. Make more work calls.

6. Learn to communicate better with the ones I love.

Long Term Goals

1. Go on a book tour.

2. Speak publically on "Dating Our Money."

3. Get married.

4. Always be patient, and never lose my temper with my kids.

5. Always have a "voice" for women, and be confident no matter what happens in life.

6. Be wealthy—emotionally and financially.

7. Buy the kitchen table I always wanted.

8. Go to Europe with my kids.

9. Tell everyone I care about how much I love and appreciate them.

10. Thank each reader of this book for caring about themselves enough to read this. Writing is what I love to do, so thank you for letting me do what I love.

So where do we go from here? We can change our world one step at a time. This book has been a journey for me. I have lived in a small cabin in the majestic mountains of North Carolina while this book was completed. Just like you, there are a thousand other things I could have done with my time without kids. Yes, you should see my house right now. It needs some love, but this was the best thing I have ever done. I made a goal, stuck with it, accomplished it. If the book never makes it to the bestseller list, oh well. The journey has been worth it. I feel a new confidence and sense that I can take on anything.

Women, find your passion and pursue it. What does it take to pursue a dream? It takes money and time. This book has given you the keys to effectively meet these challenges. No dream happens overnight, but it unfolds by small steps along the way. This book can be the beginning of your journey to wealth *now*. You deserve only happiness and wealth in life. Surround yourself with people who inspire you. Anyone who calls my cellular phone hears this message: "Surround yourself with people who inspire you."

This spring, I learned to draw a clear line in dating. If you don't inspire me, then we both need to move on. I want someone who has the courage to follow their dreams and encourage me to do the same. Recently, a guy asked me what qualities I wanted in a husband. I told him someone who thinks BIG. They have to think bigger than themselves. It sounds stupid but if they don't recycle, then I don't want them in my life. Why? They don't care enough to think about the next generation. They don't care about the earth enough to try to protect it for the future of our children, and our children's children, and many more to come.

It's your time to think big. I want you to surround yourself with people who will push you towards your dreams and hold you accountable. This requires setting goals, sticking with them and achieving them. A goal is useless if it doesn't take flight in your thought and action. This discipline of goal-setting and goal-keeping will give you the tools you need for success in life. You may not make it to the Olympics or get on the Oprah show, but your goals are just as important as anyone else's. You just need to have the courage to develop your goals and tell others your goals so they hold you accountable. Then go for it and don't let obstacles stop you!

Remember that often when you are about to achieve something great, there is something or someone to lure you off course. When I was only three months from completing this book, I had to leave my job. Why? Because there is a possibility that if I do public speaking surrounding this book, I might say something that could be financially non-compliant. (I can't imagine!) So I have had to make a huge leap of faith quitting my job in hopes that this book will be a success. I then was offered another amazing job that would supplement my income, but it was in a whole new industry. Near the end of the negotiations, the prospective employer also said to me that I could not do both. It was a start-up company and demanded all my time. It was either the book or this job. YIKES! It is scary to step out on a ledge alone, but every great leader or successful person in history has had to believe in themselves first before others could.

Toot your own horn. It is okay. Please don't get yourself in a relationship or job where you are not appreciated! It can be very demoralizing when someone you work for, or trust, calls you or abuses you emotionally. I remember hearing that emotional abuse can often be more damaging than physical abuse. Women, you must protect yourself from men who try to cut you down. It has been a long journey back to find myself and have the courage to have a voice. I am here to promise you that you can come back stronger than ever! Don't let anyone do it again to you. You are beautiful—inside and out. I know it and you need to know it also.

Well, my friends all joke with me about when will I be writing a book called "Marrying Our Money." I wish I knew. I leave that one up to God, but I am learning that the journey can be just as much fun as the destination. While writing this book, I have taken some courageous steps that I never would have imagined. If it is true that you find someone when you least expect it, then maybe my story will have a happy ending. I met a guy on an airplane who lives half-way across the country from me. Humanly it would seem absolutely insane. I am not moving any time soon, and I assume he isn't either. I am not trying to jump five steps ahead this time. He is flying out this weekend to visit. You'll have to read the next book to see what happens!

Today, step out on a limb and make some changes. I bet they will lead you closer down the path of emotional and financial peace! Enjoy the ride and don't forget it is all right to strut your stuff. Girls, go get your high heels on and kick it up! Never forget to wear your best asset—self-confidence! Now . . . Party on!

Valuable Questions From Readers

How do I save money when I have no extra cash available?

This is a question I receive regularly from others. While getting my car serviced recently, I learned of a new product that I was unaware of. Fidelity Investments now offers a credit card (with no annual fee) entitled "Fidelity Investment Rewards Visa Signature" that enables one to use a credit card and still save money. For every $100 spent on your credit card, Fidelity puts $1.50 into a Fidelity savings, IRA or 401k account. After you spend $15,000 in a year using your Fidelity credit card, the amount rises to 2% or $2 for every $100 spent.

Please know that I am not encouraging the use of credit cards but they seem engrained in people's lifestyles. This is one way that hopefully you can shop wisely and save. Remember that this card can only be used with a Fidelity account. Fidelity is one of the most recognized names in the financial world so

I would not be concerned that the company will not be around when it is time for you to retire.

Should I date a guy who is about to declare bankruptcy?

I cannot make that choice for you but am happy to give you some guidance. In these economic times, many good people have fallen into unexpected difficulties. I am sure that this is true for the man you are referring to. What I would want to know is how open is he with discussing his financial situation? Has he become wiser and is he creating a plan so this does not happen again the future? Is he asking you to lend him money so he can get on his feet again? Has he really stopped spending on miscellaneous items like expensive coffee and eating out? If you feel like he is changing, taking accountability for his actions, not draining you emotionally or financially, then I would say yes. Please remember though that you don't want to date someone with the "poor me" mentality or it will soon wear you down. Hope this helps and remember there are always "plenty of fish." (LOL, if you read my book you will learn that I used that website.)

I am so sick of constantly receiving credit card offers in the mail, how do I stop it?

Great question! One of the main ways that identity theft occurs is from people stealing credit card offers and getting your personal information and using it falsely. To be proactive, you can call and get yourself removed from pre-approved offers. You can call 888-567-8688 or go to www.optoutprescreen.com to do the same. To eliminate annoying telemarketers, please call the national do not call registry. I have my cell-phone number listed also on the do not call registry. My ten year old received a pre-approved credit card offer last weekend so it is important to stop it now!

Should I marry a guy even if he won't agree to a pre-nup?

Thank you for having the courage to ask this question! I know this is a heated topic for many. In the book I asked each reader to write a list of non-negotiables in their future mate. As a financial planner, a pre-nup is a non-negotiable item, especially now that I have kids. A pre-nup is a protection for my children that no one can touch what is meant for their future, including college education. Unfortunately, I have heard many tales of men who make a habit of preying on women's insecurities of "being along forever." These men marry women and then run off shortly after with half or more of a woman's wealth and leaving very little for her children.

Each case is so individual that it is hard for me to make a blanket statement. I think you need to see why your mate feels so strongly on this issue. Please remember if they are not willing to compromise and listen to you on this subject that these are huge "red flags" for the future. In the marriage, he may soon become this adamant on you not knowing about the finances or on how many kids you will have. You need to "trust your gut!" Women's intuitions are usually always right. There will be even bigger issues you will face when you are married so making sure you can lovingly communicate and confront, not avoid, this issue are key indicators of the success of your relationship in the future. Good Luck!

I really like this guy on the inside but he is not as "picture perfect" as I expected. What should I do?

You have no idea how often this idea is brought up. Life doesn't always give you exactly what you want or expect. I sure didn't expect my husband to pass on. When I was troubled about dating someone not picture perfect, my friend shared her experience of how she fell for her husband but he was around 3 or four inches shorter than her. She wasn't sure if she could live with it. She really had to ask herself and evaluate what mattered in life. After dating now a lot, I have realized I rarely want to date the "cutest" guy in the room because they are often very self-centered and shallow. Finding the not so picture perfect person often leads to the longest and lasting relationships. Please note that I am not asking you to settle. You have the right to your ultimate happiness. You must have chemistry for a long-term relationship to work but we often are asked to sacrifice the pretty boy for the dependable, charming and reliable husband. You may not be looking for marriage so it is alright to date only pretty boys. One of my best friends is clear that she will only marry a guy who is less attractive than her because she wants him to always have eyes for her and be grateful he found her and only her! Remember there is no perfect recipe for love.

Accountability Calendar

Four Months

Month One

Week One

- ○ Buy a money journal. Begin tracking your daily expenses.
- ○ Complete the Personal Evaluation. (Page 17)

Week Two

- ○ Write Top Five Financial Goals. (Page 27)
- ○ Evaluate Ten Common Money Mistakes Women Make.

  (Pages 29 & 30)

Are you making any of them?

How can you change your spending habits?

Week Three

- ° Complete credit card self-examination. (Page 35)
- ° Find Your Fico Score.
- ° Develop a plan to protect yourself from identity theft.

Week Four

- ° Find Accountability Partner. (Page 49)
- ° Create plan to Achieve Goals. (Page 51)

Month Two

Week Five

- ° Decide whether you want to work with a financial planner or handle investing and research on your own.
- ° Call and set up an interview with 2 or 3 financial planners if you want to use a financial planner.

(Potential questions to ask a financial planner listed on page 58&59)

Week Six

    o   Evaluate your time each day. Are you wasting too much time worrying about things you can't change? How much time do you spend on Facebook or internet dating sites? How could you use your time more wisely to support your future goals?

Week Seven

    o   Look at your portfolio. Is there asset allocation? (Research has shown that 90% of a portfolio's return is based on asset allocation over time. Page 74)

Week Eight

    o   Look at what insurance products you own. Are you and your family protected if the unexpected occurs like the death of a spouse?

    o   Buy more insurance if needed.

<u>Month Three</u>

Week Nine

- ° Start a tough conversation about money with your partner, spouse or family member.
- ° Make sure you can answer the questions about a loved one listed on page 105 & 106.

Week Ten

- ° Update or get proper legal documents for yourself and your family (if needed).

Week Eleven

- ° Create a workable budget.
- ° Look at your money journal to track ALL your expenses.

Week Twelve

- ° Face one of your fears directly like possibly approaching a cute guy in a bar or giving a speech in public at Toastmasters.

Month Four

Week Thirteen

- ° Create a savings plan for retirement.
- ° Decide how much money to put into savings like 401(k) or Roth IRA each month. (Your goal is 15% of your salary at least!)
- ° Find beverage savings calculators and coffee calculators on the internet so you can see how much you (and your family) approximately spend on these per year.

Week Fourteen

- ° Evaluate your home mortgage.
- ° Would your credit score allow you to refinance at a better score?
- ° Are you sure you have a fixed rate that doesn't balloon?
- ° Should you extend your mortgage from 15 to 30 years for tax advantages?

- ○ Do you need to move to a smaller place because your mortgage payments are eating up too much of your paycheck?
- ○ Can you get a better rate on home insurance? (Try shopping around for rates.)

Week Fifteen

- ○ Watch the movie "Pursuit of Happyness".
- ○ Make a commitment to never stop learning.
- ○ Read one money magazine, book or website each month (minimum).

Week Sixteen

- ○ Find your passion and create a plan so you can pursue it.
- ○ Make positive changes (like eliminating a relationship not going anywhere) to reach your long-term goals.
- ○ Surround yourself with people to empower you to think BIG!

'Tis the Season for Saving: 17 Tips to Keep Your Holiday Spending Habits off the Naughty List

The holidays are upon us and in addition to festive time spent with family and friends for most of us it means a lot of money spent on holiday gifts and other once-a-year expenses. Don't let this year's holiday spending ruin all of the saving you've done throughout the year. Here are valuable tips on how to keep your holiday spending in check.

Holiday shopping is about to kick into full swing. And though many Americans are saving more throughout the year, the holidays offer that all-too-tempting opportunity to let loose and splurge a little. In fact, if you aren't careful, in November and December you can blow all the good saving intentions you held firm to during the rest of the year. Last year, *Consumer Reports* found that as of October of 2010 14 million Americans were still paying off credit card charges incurred during the 2009 holiday season. This year, reports Gallup, Americans plan to spend an average of $764 on Christmas.

And while that number is still down from pre-recession amounts, it represents a significant chunk of change for many American families. In order to curb our bad spending habits during the holidays, we must first understand why we let ourselves splurge in the first place.

We spend a lot during the holidays because we love giving to our friends and family. Watching someone you love open that perfect gift can be really gratifying. The holidays also give us a guilt-free pass to shop 'til we drop. You don't have to feel bad about spending because you're not buying things for yourself, or at least you shouldn't be! And you can justify it by telling yourself, "Well, I have to get gifts for everyone or they'll be disappointed in me!" This psychology of gift giving isn't good for your financial health.

While it's nice to give someone something they want, that good feeling will quickly fade when you see how much your holiday spending affected your finances. The good news is that with careful planning you can give everyone on your list a special holiday without having to pay for it for months and months to come.

Listed below are tips on how to keep your spending and your sanity in check this holiday season:

1. Get real with yourself about your financials. Before you even make your gift list, you need to have a heart to heart with yourself about your financials. Look at how much you can realistically spend. Then decide whether or not you really need to spend that amount. If it has you feeling anxious, then absolutely create a budget that has you spending less. Think about your long-term financial plans. Don't allow your holiday spending to negatively affect your bigger plans. When you know what your financial picture really looks like, instead of thinking about it as a black hole, you'll be more inclined to control your spending.

2. Don't fall back on old holiday spending habits. When you're making your budget, it's important to remember that spending during the holidays does not stop with gifts. We allow ourselves a little more leeway when it comes to other discretionary spending, as well.

Holiday incidentals include additional food spending, entertainment costs, clothes buying, wrapping paper, and on and on. All of these costs add up, big time, and they often get overlooked during the holidays. They can also be slightly easier to eliminate or reduce than the money you're spending on gifts. For example, it isn't necessary to buy a brand new dress for your office party. You could borrow a dress from someone or add an accessory or a great pair of shoes to a dress you already own. In fact, this is actually a great reason to organize your closet. When you can easily see what you have, you can quickly put together a great holiday outfit without spending a dime. As for food costs, if you're having a holiday party, make it pot luck so you don't carry the food cost burden all by yourself.

3. Don't shop when you've got the holiday blues. This time of year can bring a lot of joy, but the hectic nature of the season can also be overwhelming. Avoid shopping when you're having a down day. Studies have shown that we are willing to spend more when we are sad. So when you're suffering from the holiday blues, curl up and watch a holiday movie or go do something fun with your kids instead. Save the shopping for a better mood.

4. Remember, 'tis the season for relationships. It's perfectly natural to want to give back to those who give to you, but it's quite possible that your friends and family will appreciate an end to spending this holiday season just as much as you. Suggest to those on your gift list that you all spend valuable time with one another rather than purchasing gifts this year. For example, suggest to your best friend an afternoon together meeting for coffee and going to a movie. Or treat your parents to a home-cooked meal and some Christmas carols performed by their grandkids.

I think you'll find that people will like the idea of making the holiday about relationships rather than shopping and spending.

And this plan will start showing dividends early on. While you and your friends and family are enjoying quality time together, you'll also be avoiding the stressful hustle and bustle that all of the holiday shoppers are suffering through. You can also take this a step further and make it even more gratifying for everyone involved. Suggest to your loved ones that the time you spend together be used to volunteer for a local charity—a great way to enjoy the true spirit of the season!

5. Establish an "Operation Holiday" plan. If there is no avoiding holiday shopping for you, once you know what your budget is start mapping out your shopping plan. Make the gift list and then think about where you'll need to go to purchase each present. Keep your key goals in mind. For example, are you trying to keep each gift under X amount of dollars? Do you want to be finished by a certain time? Avoid a certain shopping area? Again, if you stick perfectly to your plan, I think it's okay to reward yourself. Just don't go overboard. For example, if I meet my goal of buying my gifts and staying on budget, I'll treat myself to a pedicure.

6. Finish your shopping early in the season. Though getting out for those late night/early morning hours on Black Friday might not be your thing, it is best to start your holiday shopping as many shopping days before Christmas as you can.

As the holiday gets closer and you realize you haven't even made a dent in your list, you'll start to get desperate. And when you're desperate, you won't have as many misgivings about going over budget in order to get your shopping done. You'll also have less time to finish your shopping so you'll think you have to get whatever is available. 'Shop early and save' should be your new motto. Another positive to getting all your shopping out of the way early is that it gives you more time to kick back and enjoy all of the fun festivities leading up to the holidays.

7. Set a holiday shopping curfew. You don't have to go tearing through stores pushing innocent shoppers from your path, but setting a time limit on your shopping will help you stay on budget.

Keeping in mind that you need to be done by your self-imposed shopping curfew will prevent you from lingering in sections of a store that may have caught your eye but don't contain any items from your list. It will also help prevent you from spending time shopping for yourself. And because holiday shopping should be fun, take a moment to reward yourself if you do finish by your deadline. Buy yourself a cup of hot chocolate or better yet, make some for yourself and the kids when you get home. Remember, the less time you spend shopping, the more time you'll have to spend with friends and family.

8. Remember, it's the thought that counts. You might find the perfect gift for someone but then reject it because you don't think the price is significant enough to be an adequate gift.

The reality is that a gift with a lot of thought behind it or shared meaning for you and the person you're buying for can have a lot more significance than a more expensive gift. For example, a special photo of you and a friend in a frame with a special note about how much you enjoyed the time you spent together is a great gift. Or have your kids write down the 10 things they love about their grandparents and include the list in a photo album of the kids. These are all gifts that involve more thought and meaning than just going to the store and buying a gift. And the people receiving them will truly appreciate it.

9. Make a list, check it twice, and bring cash! How many times have you walked in a store and immediately found the perfect gift for a friend? Sure, you hadn't planned on spending that much, but she would love it, so why not? You can just put it on your credit card, right? Wrong! If you use your credit card, you'll probably end up buying that gift for your friend two or three times over in interest payments. Do not stray from your list. If you do stray, the cost of the non-list item needs to be the same as the one you had already budgeted. Only bring cash with you when you're shopping so you can stay within your budget.

10. Save merrily by trading in your rewards points for gifts or gift cards. You should always, always use your credit cards wisely. Never make purchases on your credit card unless you can pay them off at the end of the month. And during the holidays avoid whipping them out to pay for gifts. But one positive role credit cards can have during the holidays is rewards points.

A few years ago, I bought my sister a chair she wanted from Pottery Barn using rewards points. I redeemed some of my points for a Pottery Barn gift card and then used it to buy her the chair. In fact, I save up all my rewards points throughout year and use them in December for gifts. Another example, teacher gifts. I always get my kids' teachers Barnes & Noble gift cards using redeemed points.

11. Point, click and save. The benefits of online shopping are obvious. You don't have to battle holiday traffic, it is practically hassle free and it's easier to compare prices. The prices are also almost always better online. You have a greater selection and usually free shipping is offered around the holidays. And when you use specific search terms, you can avoid being distracted by all of the other items you might want to look at or be tempted to buy if you were shopping in the store."

12. Don't shop for yourself. According to Lab42, last year the average holiday shopper spent $107.50 on themselves. When you're making it ok for yourself to do a lot of spending, it can be difficult not to stray off your list and buy a couple of things for yourself.

We have all done it. You see something you like and think, 'Wow, that is so cute. I will buy one for so-and-so and one for me.' You can resist this urge by implementing some of the tips we've already covered, but also by keeping in mind that you'll be receiving gifts at Christmas. They'll be all the more special if you haven't been buying yourself new things all along. Also, keep in mind that you'll be finding the best deals after Christmas. So wait until you can get more bang for your buck.

13. Don't shop with a holiday budget saboteur. If you prefer doing your shopping with someone else in tow, be sure to choose someone who won't encourage you to go off budget.

I can whiz in and out of a mall in 30 minutes if I'm with my son who hates shopping or bring a girlfriend and be there half a day.

Carefully consider who you're shopping with. Will the person encourage unexpected buying or splurging? If so, you might want to politely decline their invitation. You might also consider who's going to keep you on track. You might bring along one of your kids because you know you want to show them how to be fiscally responsible and use the opportunity to show them how to stick to a budget.

14. Have a secret Santa-style gift exchange. Depending on the size of your family, buying a gift for each family member can be daunting, especially when you only see some of them once a year!

There are exceptions but I think by and large once you reach a certain age—specifically the age where you feel obligated to buy gifts for everyone—the reality of gift giving and receiving sets in. My point is that most of the adults in your family will probably be grateful not to have to buy a gift for everyone. Instead, suggest that your family do a gift exchange. At Thanksgiving, have everyone pick a name out of a hat. Then, you only buy for that person. It is a great way to help everyone cut down on unneeded spending. And if you're just shopping for one, it gives you a lot more time to think about what would make the best gift.

15. Don't be afraid to re-gift. Take an inventory of re-gifting possibilities. Are there any gift cards you've never used? Any clothes hanging in your closet with the tags still on them? Any gifts you've received in years passed that you've never taken out of the box? If so, you might want to consider re-gifting them.

Many people avoid re-gifting because they think it violates some rule of etiquette. But when done properly, it can help you find a home for items that you're never going to use. Sure, there is a line that has to be drawn. If your grandmother got you a sweater that you hate, but she expects to see you wearing it then that's probably not an item that you should re-gift. But let's say a former colleague got you a scarf as part of a Secret Santa exchange at work last year. It's a perfectly nice scarf, but it's a color that just doesn't look good on you. That's a great item to re-gift. You'll get it out of your house and someone else will love having it."

16. Make like Santa's elves and DIY. Getting crafty during the holidays is fun and can save you a lot of money on gifts. There are any number of options depending on your level of craftiness. Costco has cute jars filled with cookie dough ingredients. We could all do that at home! Bake cookies and place them in a holiday tin for your kids' teachers. Frame your kids' artwork for their grandparents. The possibilities are truly endless and truly cost-effective!

17. If you're super savvy, plan (way) ahead. As we've touched on above, there are always great deals after Christmas. That means if you can get over your holiday hangover fast enough, you can get a jump start on buying gifts for next year while also saving a bundle. My bargain shopper friend buys many of her gifts for the next year's Christmas during the current year's after-holiday sales. She is always done shopping by October. If immediately after Christmas is too soon for you to think about the next year, take advantage of other sales throughout the year. For example, there are almost always great sales at Easter, the 4th of July, Labor Day and Memorial Day.

We naturally want to give during the holidays. But what's important to remember is that you can give a lot without spending a lot. Don't put a price tag on your holidays. Stick to your budget and then be generous with your time and spirit. Once the holidays are over, you'll be happy you didn't blow your savings and you and your family and friends will be fulfilled by the time you all spent together.